From Orange To Singapore

From Orange To Singapore

* * *

A Shipyard Builds a Legacy

Paul A. Mattingly Jr.

© 2017 Paul A. Mattingly, Jr.
All rights reserved.

ISBN: 1484858247
ISBN 13: 9781484858240

Contents

	Prologue	ix
1	Orange, Texas	1
2	*Sea Otter II*, "That Stinker"	8
3	World War II	13
4	Banana Republic: The Bednar Story	18
5	Tugboats and "SPAM" for Russia	30
6	Levingston's Training Program	39
7	The Cajuns Come to Orange	43
8	Talent	52
9	Lake Maracaibo, Venezuela	65
10	New York Harbor	69
11	The *John F. Kennedy*	73
12	What Happened with Iran	79
13	Pioneering Marine Offshore Rigs	85
14	Herbert Hunt	97
15	The "Cadillac" of Rigs	103
16	Mohole	126
17	Brown & Root Awarded Contract	130

18	Mohole Is No Hole	133
19	Scripps and Levingston	141
20	From Ashes of Disaster Grow the Roses of Success	146
21	Inward-Looking Telescope	152
22	Miracle of the Computer	163
23	*Hughes Glomar Explorer* Inspired by the *Glomar Challenger*	174
24	Cecil H. Green	187
25	Levingston Goes to Singapore	194
26	Roy Huffington	207
27	The End of an Era	212
28	Rocket 88	219
29	The Final Days of Levingston	223
30	David W. Hannah, Jr.	227
31	College Students and Levingston	230
32	Conclusion	234
	Partial List of Bibliography	237

To my loving wife of 52 years, Carole, who has supported me in a four-year project of research - traveling with me, helping with interviews, making suggestions and proofreading this book. Her contribution has been extraordinary.

To my daughters, Michelle and Jennifer, and their husbands, Ernie and John, who have patiently listened to my Levingston stories and given me encouragement.

To my five grandchildren – Travis, Mary Margaret, John, Caroline and Christina, who have loved me unconditionally and have supplied me with the impetus to continue writing this historical documentation.

To the memory of my parents, Paul Allen and Maureen Kelly Mattingly, who lived the Levingston story. I hope they know of my literary endeavor, and I hope they are proud.

Above all, in loving memory of my beloved son, John Kelly Mattingly, who left this earth far too soon. I can continually hear him saying, "Keep going, Dad!"

To my seven younger brothers: Joseph, Walter (deceased), Timothy, Edward, Kevin, Stephen, and Gregory. We are a clan of strong siblings and proud to be Mattinglys. Thank you for listening to my "book tales" prior to publication.

To all those who shared stories and information with me, you have been invaluable in the writing of this book. You know who you are, and I thank you all so very much!

Prologue

Throughout childhood, I sat at the feet of shipbuilding giants, the visionaries who built the Levingston Shipbuilding Company. Though the company germinated and grew in the small, historical lumber town of Orange, Texas, the sweep of its engineering feats and construction marvels is ongoing and global. In its wake, the company left a trained workforce of "can-do" daredevils who, to this day, are still dispatched to resolve dangerous situations all over the world.

I have spent much time analyzing why this lean company in an out-of-the-way Texas town could produce and sustain such firepower. Even though I acknowledge that the public at large does not really relate to shipbuilders, I believe that *From Orange to Singapore* has a great deal going for it. The "can-do" spirit carried Levingston into unbelievable adventures, the stories of which should amaze and entertain the reader.

On the trail of my tale about Levingston Shipbuilding, I discovered the rush of an unexpected discovery about the *Glomar Challenger* in the book, *"The CIA's Greatest Covert*

ix

Paul A. Mattingly Jr.

Operation: Inside the Daring Mission to Recover a Nuclear-armed Soviet Sub, by David H. Sharp. According to Sharp, "There are small but great moments in history when some few have dared to do the impossible. This book is a record of one of those moments. Project Azorian - the monumentally audacious six-year mission to recover the sub and learn its secrets - has been celebrated within the CIA as its greatest covert operation. It was the ship, *Hughes Glomar Explorer.*"

Interestingly, there were no engineered specifications given to Global Marine, Inc. in Port Arthur, Texas, the builder of the *Hughes Glomar Explorer.* The CIA told Global Marine what they wanted and left the design and construction to them. John Graham, designer of the *Hughes Glomar Explorer,* and Curtis Crooke of Global Marine had also directed the construction of the Levingston-built *Glomar Challenger.* Sharp writes, "The special CIA team set up to initially decide how to raise the *K-129* (Russian sub) was drawn to Global Marine, Inc. because of the operational capability of the new *Glomar Challenger.* This was needed to keep the ship hovering over the *K-129,* located three miles below (16,500 ft.) the waterline. Global Marine arranged for a tour of the *Glomar Challenger* for several of the CIA Headquarters' teams. After the tour, most of the team agreed that Global Marine had a place in their future.

Sharp was head of the CIA team. This verifies that the *Glomar Challenger* was the inspiration for the *Hughes Glomar Explorer.* Per Sharp, he, "using an alias identity, managed the eighty-five-man program office in Los Angeles that was responsible for directing the sea trials and integrated system testing of the ship (*Hughes Glomar Explorer*) and the claw that would be used to capture the sunken submarine." The operation, code-named "Project Azorian," was so secret, its existence was not declassified until February 2010, and much of the data is still top-secret.

To this day, many of the files, photographs, videotapes, and other documentary evidence remain closed to the public. The costs have never been revealed. Estimates have ranged as high as an "unbelievable" $800 million, which in 2016 dollars would be $4.8 billion. The author was one of the principal CIA operatives involved in the mission and probably one of the few who has all the notes and documents to tell the tale as to what really happened, that is, at least as much as the CIA editorial staff would permit him to print. Also in 2006, the American Society of Mechanical Engineers declared the *Hughes Glomar Explorer* to be a "National Historic Mechanical Engineering Landmark," claiming that the recovery system was the greatest marine engineering accomplishment of the Twentieth Century. Yet, the story of the *Glomar Challenger*, the predecessor of the *Hughes Glomar Explorer*, is an even greater thrill of discovery. It became a milestone in ocean research. Its mother vessel, the HMS *Challenger*, in its expedition of 1872-76, is credited with giving birth to the study of oceanography, the branch of earth science that studies the ocean. The legacy of the *Glomar Challenger*'s drilling includes validating the theory of plate tectonics and tracing Earth's changing climate back 100 million years, as well as inventing the field of paleoceanography, the study of the story of the oceans' circulation, chemistry, biogeography, fertility, and sedimentation.

The evidence of the deep-water ocean research is reflected in the 21-story oceanography structure at MIT, the Cecil and Ida Green Building, built in 1965. Mr. Green, co-founder of Texas Instruments, received both his bachelor's and master's degrees from MIT. Texas A&M University later built a 15-story oceanography building in 1972 on their campus at College Station, Texas.

From designing and building ocean rescue tugs during WWII, Levingston converted to the post-war construction of off-shore drilling rigs, becoming known as the "oil industry's shipyard." The company also built ferry boats for Lake Maracaibo in Venezuela and for New York City's Staten Island fleet. The ferry boat, *John F. Kennedy*, continues to transport passengers between Manhattan and Staten Island. Today, Levingston's legacy lives on in the Singapore-based shipyard known as Keppel FELS – Far East Levingston Shipbuilding – founded in 1969. It is the world's largest builder of movable jackup rigs.

With these tales of shipbuilding and vessels of various kinds, I hope to inspire the thrill of the oceans, both as means of transportation and of exploration of the waters that gave birth to life itself. We ride the waves and we learn and benefit from the oceans that create them!

1
Orange, Texas

The story of Orange, Texas, begins on the banks of the Sabine River at a location situated a hundred miles east of Houston and thirty miles east of the fabled Spindletop oilfield, discovered in 1901. The tri-cities of Orange, Port Arthur, and Beaumont are known as the "Texas Golden Triangle." Here, Texas braggadocio and hospitality meet the Cajun *joie de vivre*. On no place did World War II have a bigger impact than in the small town of Orange with a population of 7,000 people.

Lumbering had been the primary economic driver of the town since the beginning of the twentieth century. Numerous mansions sprang up on the main street, Green Avenue, during that time. Family members and executives of the Lutcher and Moore Lumber Company built most, including the W. H. Stark mansion (1895), one of the finest examples of Queen Anne architecture.

It was said one could drive across the state of Louisiana from the Sabine River bordering Texas to the Mississippi River and never get out of sight of land owned by Lutcher and Moore Lumber Company. It was also reported that in the late nineteenth century, Henry Lutcher and G. B. Moore owned 1.5 million acres in Louisiana and Texas. The early to mid-1920's is generally considered the ending date of the great lumber boom, for it was then that almost all of the big mills had run out of timber. At one time the Lutcher and Moore Lumber Company was reputed to be the largest lumbering concern in the nation.

Lutcher had bought Moore's interests in their mutual company in 1907. After that transaction, the company came totally under the control of Henry Jacob Lutcher and his wife, Miriam. They had two daughters, one married to Bill Stark and the other married to Dr. E. W. Brown, Jr. Lutcher's health deteriorated, and he died in a sanitarium in Cincinnati, Ohio, in 1912. Following the deaths of his wife and two daughters, Lutcher's fortune was divided among his four grandchildren: William Henry Stark, Lutcher Brown, E. W. Brown, Jr., and Mrs. R.A. Moore, mother of Babette Odom.

Orange, Texas, became a boom town at the turn of the century, spawned by outrageous fortune: the legendary Spindletop oil find. In 1901, the crest of a salt dome in Texas flatlands blew, producing a world record geyser reaching 150 feet height and spewing approximately 100,000 barrels of oil for nine days. Wildcatters called it "black gold." This "gusher," as Texans still refer to it, is widely considered the birth of the modern oil industry. Spindletop, only thirty miles from Orange, had drawn thousands to the area and enhanced the populations of nearby Beaumont and Port Arthur, Texas. The three cities eventually became known as "The Golden Triangle," not only for the black gold the oilfields produced, but also because of the golden glow generated by scores of area refineries—quite a geometric sight from a nighttime flight.

Even in 1919, the area exuded a peculiar energy. Just across the river lay Louisiana, with its robust French Acadian population ready to be tapped and challenged. Just a hundred miles up the road, the fast-growing city of Houston (population 138,000) pulsated with the energy of the oil business while Orange was changing to an oil economy from its long-entrenched lumber businesses. Here, in the oil belt, the locals were used to fortunes waxing and waning, feast or famine, boom or bust. Folks understood: if they did not risk, they might not eat.

Captain George Levingston liked the odds. He saw a way to service both the oil and the lumber business by building wooden tugboats and barges. The son of an Irish immigrant, Levingston established his company in the southeastern-most corner of Texas on a five-acre tract of land where thick piney woods give way to river banks and marshlands. For a time, the company prospered, but by 1933, it needed bailing out. Edgar W. Brown, Jr., grandson of the wealthy lumber baron, H. J. Lutcher, kept Levingston afloat by acquiring 80 percent ownership. More importantly, Edgar Brown brought the company the new vision that would carry it through the next half century.

Brown already owned a related barge-towing company, Hitman Towing Co., and he was involved in numerous and diverse businesses. He wanted to make Levingston a first-class shipyard, powered by the best talent he could find, people of energy and enthusiasm. He could recruit extraordinarily talented young people and forge them into a team. He wanted the little shipyard to do great things and the people to have fun doing it.

Many of his fun-loving employees were Louisiana "Cajuns," a culture known for producing lively spirits with a penchant for hard work and risk taking. Along with others of varying ancestry, the Cajuns left their stamp on the shipbuilding industry. The "can-do" spirit of their approach to shipbuilding is their legacy.

Fun was no obstacle in 1930's and 1940's Orange. Gambling casinos abounded to the east, just across the Sabine River Bridge. In the Louisiana swamplands, gambling had taken root uncurtailed. The seven casinos lining Highway 90 were referred to as "across the river." There, awaited bands, nightclub acts, dice, roulette wheels, blackjack gambling, daily race results, and fast friendships. The farthest and most prestigious was the lavishly decorated Grove Dining Club, with two formal dining rooms seating a total of 700. When you went to the Grove, you dressed in your best.

The Grove advertised itself as "The South's Finest Dinner Club, Famous from Coast to Coast." To get to the Grove, it was necessary to cross over the Highway 90 two-lane bridge (formerly the Old Spanish Trail) connecting Orange to Louisiana. The crossing put travelers in the Louisiana swamps where approximately seven gambling casinos lined the highway. The Grove, owned and run by Marian and Sam Smith, was the last one, about four miles from Orange.

The most unique casino was the *Harry Lee*, a stern-wheel steamer originally owned by the Lee Line out of Memphis. It had once plied the waters of the Mississippi River and had a great steel hull that measured 180 feet by 39 feet in width with three levels. New owner Claude Williams renamed the vessel, *Showboat,* and displayed the name in large lettering. It was tied up on a canal with a gangplank to land next to Highway 90. When the road was cut off by the new Interstate 10 located to the north, the *Showboat* was moved to the Mississippi River and pulled up to Chicago in 1953.

Another gambling dinner club was named DeMary's after the owner, Felix Joseph DeMary, a Louisiana Frenchman from Abbeville, Louisiana. He owned a small interest in the famous Balinese Room nightclub in Galveston, Texas. The Balinese Room belonged to the Maceo family whose descendants continue to operate casinos in Las Vegas, among which is a chain called Stations Casino. Galveston native and Maceo family descendant, Tillman Fertitta, owns the Golden Nugget Hotels and Casinos in both Las Vegas and Lake Charles.

DeMary also provided wire service for gambling casinos in the State of Texas. DeMary's Louisiana operation obtained racing information from a wire service controlled by the Carlos Marcello family in New Orleans. DeMary had contracted with Sam Maceo to transmit the information to Maceo's Turf Grill in Galveston via a direct telephone hookup.

On the outskirts of Orange, DeMary owned a farm with a stable and full racetrack where he trained his thoroughbred racehorses. The farm had a railroad siding that he used to load his horses for transportation to out-of-town racetracks. The most popular destination was New Orleans and the Fair Grounds Race Course that first opened in 1852. It is said that DeMary lost a ton of money operating his racehorse stables.

Another club was owned by a New Orleans man who moved to Orange for retirement and named his establishment the Flamingo Club. It was located next to Felix DeMary's dinner club. The rumor is that he had invested in the Flamingo Club in Las Vegas and named the Orange casino after his Vegas investment.

The offshore marine industry was filled with some of the richest and biggest gamblers in the world. When they came to the backwater town of Orange to do business at Levingston shipyard, they were assured royal treatment and limousine rides to high-stakes gambling establishments. Some Levingston shipyard workers doubled as bodyguards to give the customers a sense of security in this strange world of gambling in the swamps of Louisiana. All the casinos would treat them, the Levingston people, and their guests, with the best they had to offer. The Levingston group also had the connections to provide the same kind of services in Houston, Galveston, and New Orleans gambling casinos.

Orange, Texas, was a dry town and had been for a long time. Some say it always was. The extremes of the town's social life were unique. They ran the gamut from the hard-shelled Baptist lives of no smoking, no drinking, and no dancing to the wide-open underbelly of a festive Mardi Gras running continuously. This devil-may-care nightlife played itself out into the 1950's, when Senator Estes Kefauver, in his famous televised hearings, went after racketeering in the United States. Local lore suggests a deal was cut between the federal government and casino owners "across the river." If they agreed to shut down their gambling casinos, the federal government would not audit their tax returns. Every casino in the Orange vicinity shut down. A lot of money changed hands, with most players losing much of their savings. Finally, gambling was shut down in southeast Texas – from Orange to Port Arthur to Beaumont to Houston to Galveston. When gamblers who had frequented the local casinos started going out to Las Vegas, they felt quite at home. Many of the Vegas pit bosses and dealers were familiar faces who had migrated from their previous work in Texas.

2

Sea Otter II, "That Stinker"

Even before the Japanese attack on Pearl Harbor in December of 1941 that launched the United States into a world war, German submarines were actively targeting and sinking Allied ships crossing the Atlantic. The day after the Japanese attack on Pearl Harbor, the U.S. declared war on Japan. Three days later, on December 11, 1941, Germany and Italy declared war on the United States. Within a matter of days, the United States had been attacked by Japan and was in a state of war with Japan, Italy, and Germany.

The nation's defenses and maritime industry were ill-equipped to respond to the impending threat. The Germans clearly held the upper hand in the battle to control the supply of war materials across the seas. America's military and its civilian and industrial sectors responded to this threat with innovative technologies, emergency programs, and coordinated efforts between federal, state, and local personnel. One of the lesser-known concepts developed to confront the U-boat threat was the *Sea Otter II*, a lightweight, shallow-draft, gasoline-driven freighter, designed and built at Levingston's shipyard.

Sea Otter II, an experimental freighter, was a pet project of President Franklin Delano Roosevelt, who was known to have a love of the seas and Navy tradition. The Roosevelt family had been involved in international shipping, and he was Assistant Secretary of the Navy from 1913 to 1920. Roosevelt was uniquely qualified with international experience amid the European political unrest. Levingston completed the *Sea Otter II* project in just ninety days. And although the *Sea Otter II* was considered by many as a failure, and therefore not replicated, the experience in building this new ship on time and under difficult conditions instilled in the shipyard a "can-do" spirit that carried over into the postwar decades.

The development of the *Sea Otter II* is a whopper of a story involving Levingston, the anti-U-boat campaign, the Chrysler Corporation, and President Roosevelt. The *Sea Otter II* design embodied a novel arrangement of engine propulsion never used in oceangoing freighters. Lightweight, simple in construction, and relatively cheap both in original cost and upkeep, this craft was designed with a shallow-draft hull to counter the threat of torpedoes from enemy submarines and safely deliver war materials across the oceans without disruption from deadly German underwater prowlers.

A Levingston newsletter from the 1970's recalled the story of the *Sea Otter II* project: "Over a luncheon table one day in February 1939, two men sat discussing a type of ship that they thought could meet the challenge of a submarine." Commander Hamilton V. Bryan, USN Retired, and an automobile engineer with Chrysler by the name of Warren Noble conceived the broad outline of the ship, which would be propelled by Chrysler gas auto engines. It would be a ship for a new way to transport cargo across the Atlantic and be resistant to the deadly German U-boats. The key was the low draft of eleven feet, which would make it difficult for torpedoes to hit.

When the Navy refused to develop, and run an experimental model for the prototype, a New York lawyer raised the money for an eighty-foot-long model to be built. President Roosevelt had the British government order the first *Sea Otter II* under the lend-lease program for $350,000. The plans were incomplete, but the decision was made to have it built as an experimental freighter/tanker class with Eads Johnson, a famous marine architect, to design the ship and oversee the production.

The first requirement of the designers was to create a craft of shallow draft, at low cost, which could be produced in large numbers. The ship was designed to carry 1,500 tons of cargo. With its relatively small size, the ship could be built at inland yards and taken to sea by way of rivers or ship channels. The real revolution in design, however, was in the application of power and an all-welded steel hull, one of the first wartime vessels built using this new technology.

When the Navy put the *Sea Otter II* concept out for bid, one of the requirements was to build it in fewer than ninety days. Apparently, none of the Navy shipyards or any other shipyards across the country wanted the contract, despite the fact it was cost-plus. Levingston, one of the few shipyards with experience in welding steel plates, took the job. Up to that point, the shipyard had experience in managing and building steel-welded hulls for tugs and barges, and, therefore, seemed capable of completing this experimental craft in three months.

Levingston had all 250 employees working around the clock on the job. The ship was completed at a cost of $550,000. The 24/7 work schedule and lack of complete drawings accounted for the high cost. The *Sea Otter II* was launched on August 23, 1941. Mrs. Eads Johnson, wife of the ship's designer, christened the boat.

The *Sea Otter II* had several design innovations and flaws. It looked different from any other ship ever built, with a high-flanged bow, a small bridge, and low hatches. The hull was made of sheet-steel plates, which were produced by rolling mills and could be easily welded. It had sixteen 110-horsepower Chrysler gasoline automobile engines and four as back-up engines. The gasoline engines had no mufflers and made loud noises, which could be heard at great distances across the seas. Critics named it "that stinker." Some called it the most ridiculous vessel ever built. Columnists and congressmen wanted to know why the U.S. government had invested in such an experimental project. A congressional investigating committee considered the matter and determined that the vessel had not had a full and fair sea trial. Furthermore, Navy and Maritime Commission officials had been hostile to the sponsors of the concept.

Walter Lippmann, famed newspaper columnist, wrote several articles critical of the ship. He argued that, in a time of war, there was no justification for experimentation with a radically new idea such as the *Sea Otter II*. The small, shallow-draft, gasoline-driven freighter designed to break through the German submarine blockade in the Atlantic lacked technical capabilities and political support, especially from the U.S. Navy. Whatever the negatives of this project, the ship's unusual design and its completion time of less than ninety days gave Levingston a national reputation as a "can-do" shipbuilding company.

3

World War II

For such a small population, the community of Orange, Texas, was heavily involved in World War II. Looking at the scope of Orange's economic and social impact, we can see a clear picture of how a community benefited the nation. Over 20,000 shipyard workers descended on the town which had a population of 7,000.

In the eyes of an American, 1939 is the date given as the start of World War II. But there are millions of Chinese and Koreans who have a much earlier starting date for that war. The Nanking Massacre, also known as the Rape of Nanking, was a mass murder and war rape that occurred during the six-week period following the Japanese capture of the city of Nanking (Nanjing), the former capital of the Republic of China, on December 13, 1937. Historians and witnesses have estimated that 250,000 to 300,000 people were killed. Several of the key perpetrators of the atrocities, at the time labeled as war crimes, were later tried and found guilty at the Nanjing War Crimes Tribunal, and were subsequently executed. The reason historians give for Japan's attacking the United States is that the United States was enforcing an embargo to stop Japan's aggressive war in China.

World War II started in Europe during 1936, when Generalissimo Francisco Franco started a coup to overthrow the newly formed democratic government of Spain. Nazi Germany and Fascist Italy aggressively supported Franco. The oil for Franco's armed forces was being delivered by the Texas Company (Texaco) tankers running from the Texaco Port Arthur refinery to Spain. It is reported that Texaco illegally supplied Franco's fascist rebels in Spain, despite a federal fine, with a total 3,500,000 barrels. At the time, Congress did not want to get involved in another European war.

In 1938, Edgar Brown hired Edward Timothy Malloy, a shipyard superintendent, from a large Beaumont shipyard. Malloy was from Chicago, where he had started in the construction business with his brother, Frank. Malloy had come to Texas and started work at Todd Shipyard in Galveston. He was soon hired away to work at the Bethlehem Shipyard in Beaumont. The story goes that the owners and customers were highly impressed with Malloy, and the general manager of Bethlehem figured Malloy was a threat to his job, so he fired him. Brown quickly hired him to run Levingston.

Malloy was a lovable Irish construction man. He smoked cigars, drank whiskey, told funny and entertaining stories, cussed like a sailor, and had the charm to talk the birds out of the trees. Malloy had no children, and he came to view the shipyard workers as his family. My parents named two of my younger brothers, Timothy, and Edward, after Malloy. "Mr.

Ed," or the "old man," as he was affectionately called, provided the glue that created the family culture among the shipyard workers. He practically lived in the shipyard. He knew everybody, and anybody could walk up to him and discuss whatever they wanted.

Cats were a form of good luck in the shipbuilding industry. They also controlled rats. Malloy, too, was concerned about rats. He made sure that cats were kept around the shipyard and fed daily. Tommy Simar, who worked in the shipyard as a machinist, loved to tell the story of when Mr. Ed saw a worker throwing welding rods at a cat. Malloy didn't fire the worker, but threatened him with the loss of his job if he were ever caught again "damaging and wasting my property." Simar said, "There weren't any rats in the shipyard."

Mr. Ed's only real sign of power was the fact that he had a private Cadillac limousine driven by a chauffeur named John Reid. It was a gray color, the same color as all the Levingston cars. When R. Thomas McDermott, founder of the marine contracting company named after his father, J. Ray McDermott, rode with Mr. Malloy one day in his limousine, he immediately ordered one for himself. I remember meeting Mr. McDermott with my father and Mr. Ed. We were waiting for him at the front gate of the shipyard. Mr. McDermott was riding in the front seat with the biggest, longest cigar I had ever seen. I expected a giant of a man to step out of his Cadillac limousine. Instead, a man of very short stature appeared. Mr. McDermott and fellow Irishman Ed Malloy were close friends, and J. Ray McDermott was probably the most loyal customer Levingston ever had. Levingston built and repaired many of McDermott's pipe lay and derrick barges.

McDermott International was a loyal customer of Levingston Shipbuilding Company going back to the 1950's. Levingston built the *McDermott Derrick Barge No.23 Floating Crane*, which had a gross tonnage of 8,094 tons. The vessel was completed October 4, 1969. It was the largest vessel ever built by Levingston in Orange, Texas, with a size of 420 feet by 120 feet by 28 feet.

"Mr. Ed" loved to go to New Orleans. On weekends, he would have the Levingston-owned twin beach airplane fly him over to the Crescent City on Friday evenings. The pilot and copilot would fly back to Orange to be with their families. Then, first thing Monday morning, they flew back to New Orleans to pick him up. At the time, New Orleans was the center of the marine business for the Gulf of Mexico and the Caribbean.

Malloy believed in the importance of all the workers and worked to make them content with their jobs. When the employees also own the company, they tend to look at the company as an extension of their family. Since Malloy and his brother Frank had no children, it was easy for them to consider the people at Levingston as part of their family. He was passionate in his love of the shipyard, and it was reflected in his dealings.

I visited with him in 1965. As we walked around his front yard, looking at the blooming azaleas, he told me how much he missed my father. He said that was the most fun he ever had was working with him. Mr. Ed's wife, "Baby," died in the mid-1950's, and he married Marjorie Black, a widow. She was instrumental in persuading him to set up the Ed T. Malloy Foundation, benefiting various charitable nonprofits in Orange. In 2015 it had assets of around $6.5 million and contributes an average of $325,000 a year to the Orange community.

4

Banana Republic: The Bednar Story

The phrase *banana republic* was coined around 1904 by the American writer, O. Henry (William Sydney Porter, 1862–1910). The phrase was applied to countries run by banana companies.

One of the first big moves for Levingston Shipbuilding under the leadership of Edgar Brown was to hire a top-notch marine engineer. Brown told Ed Malloy to hire only the best. Malloy found Willard "Willie" Ulcher, chief engineer at United Fruit and Steamship Co., in New Orleans. This firm operated refrigerated ships for hauling fruits and bananas. In 1939, it also built and operated the first centrally air-conditioned cruise liner for its cruise business operating in the Gulf of Mexico.

Far left: Willie Ulcher with customers. (1950)

Ulcher graduated from high school in Albany, New York, and then entered MIT in 1926, earning a Bachelor of Science degree in naval architecture in 1930. During World War II, there were only four schools of naval architecture and marine engineering in the United States - the University of California at Berkeley, MIT, the University of Michigan, and the private Webb Institute on Long Island, New York.

Ulcher was a brilliant ship architect, ship modeler, and musician. He was also a party lover. People who came to work for Levingston would remark how old-timers would utter his name in reverence. Ulcher was known as an engineer who would always go back to first principles - if something doesn't work in terms of first principles, then it probably isn't the right solution. Of course, he had the benefit of an MIT engineering education and experience in New York working for a marine engineering firm. Ulcher also personally built the scale models of his projects. He worked for Levingston from 1938 until his death in 1951.

Paul A. Mattingly Jr.

The story of Peter Bednar gives unique insight into the people and culture of the Levingston family. Bednar was a Romanian national who was educated in Germany at the University of Munich in civil engineering. After completing his studies, Bednar left Europe in 1924 at the age of twenty-one and traveled to Cuba. His plans were to come to the United States to begin his engineering career. Instead, circumstances led him to a job in Central America with the United Fruit Company. In Honduras, Bednar worked building banana plantations, railroads, and shipping terminals. At one time, he was also a plantation manager. While there, Bednar met his wife, Francisca, a Panama native from a prominent family known for their successful Panama hat business.

During World War II, American officials persuaded their Latin American neighbors to deport thousands of ethnic Germans to the United States to be imprisoned as "enemy aliens." About 5,000 were brought to this country by the United States and incarcerated in several camps. Hundreds of the interned Latin Americans, many of whom were, by birthright, citizens of one of the republics, were exchanged for persons of the Americas held by the Third Reich; that is, they were deported to Germany.

Bednar was arrested while living in Honduras and given over to U.S. officials. He was transported to San Francisco, California, on a U.S. Army transport, which arrived on May 26, 1942. From there, Bednar was sent to Texas and held at Camp Kennedy, sixty miles southeast of San Antonio. The camp held only single men - about 1,168 Germans, 705 Japanese, 72 Italians, and 62 men from Romania and other

European countries. One of the objectives was to offer prisoners the option to be reunited with their families if they would agree to be repatriated to their country of origin in exchange for American prisoners. It is interesting to note that Germans were the largest ethnic group in America. In San Antonio, Texas, one in every six persons was of German heritage.

While working for a banana company and stationed in Honduras, Bednar had established a close friendship with Levingston's chief engineer, Willie Ulcher. United was controlled by the famed, wealthy Cabot family of Boston, but it was run by Sam "The Banana Man" Zemurray, a Jew who lived in New Orleans. One of the interesting stories about Zemurray was that when the members of the United Nations voted to deny membership to Israel in 1948, Zemurray got involved. He personally called leaders of nations he was doing business with in Central America and got them to change their vote, and Israel was voted into the United Nations. As the president of United Fruit, he was the most important man in Central America. United Fruit was one of the first truly global concerns. They operated over one hundred fifty ships carrying bananas and other products from Central America, as well as an ocean liner carrying passengers all over the Caribbean and the Gulf of Mexico. They controlled millions of acres and over a hundred thousand employees. United was the largest employer in seven Latin American countries and included the greatest fleet of refrigerated vessels in the world. It included major holdings in Cuba, where, in 1959, Fidel Castro nationalized everything United Fruit owned in Cuba. The loss to United Fruit was estimated as approaching $100 million. Castro's father had worked for United Fruit. Castro's former father-in-law represented United Fruit and their holdings in Cuba.

Castro and his wife, Mirta Diaz-Balart, had been divorced in 1955. Their only child, Fidel Angel Castro Diaz-Balart, was rumored as being groomed to replace his father. The economy was booming. It was a beautiful place. Jim Davis, the author, described it: "The famous Nacional Hotel was magnificent. The Tropicana Night Club's gambling casino was a marvel. And Cuban rum distillers had sampling stands all over the place." Cubans liked Americans and Americans liked them. But in the background, the story goes that the Batista regime was intoxicated with cleaning out bank accounts. The setting was ripe for the overthrow of the Cuban government.

Rich Cohen, author of *The Fish That Ate the Whale: The Life and Times of America's Banana King*, unveils Zemurray and his world "of banana cowboys, mercenary soldiers, Honduran peasants, CIA agents, and American statesmen." On the United Fruit board of directors was John Foster Dulles, Secretary of State under Eisenhower, and his brother, Allen Dulles, the first civilian director of the CIA. Both were famous for organizing the countries of the world to fight communism. John Foster Dulles had for three decades been a senior partner of the top Wall Street corporate law firm of Sullivan & Cromwell. Dulles's wife was Janet Pomeroy Avery, a first cousin of John D. Rockefeller, Jr.

Sam Zemurray had brought on as his public relations counsel, Edward Bernays, a man known for tapping the ideas of his uncle, Sigmund Freud, on why people behave the way they do. In 1995, Ann Douglas, a professor of English and comparative literature at Columbia University, wrote in *Terrible Honesty: Mongrel Manhattan in the 1920's*, (Farrar, Straus & Giroux) that in that era, "Freud [Sigmund] was the chosen mentor of Madison Avenue," and "Edward Bernays, often called the 'father of public relations,' who orchestrated the commercialization of a culture, was Freud's nephew and a self-conscious popularizer of his thought." Adam Curtis's award-winning 2002 documentary for the BBC, *The Century of Self*, pinpoints Bernays as the originator of modern public relations, and Bernays was named one of the 100 most influential Americans of the 20th century by *Life Magazine*. Bernays was known for his scientific technique of opinion-molding, the "engineering of consent." He was also called the "King of Spin."

One of Bernays' public relations campaigns was for United Fruit Company. He spun out a massive propaganda campaign to convince the public that Guatemala's elected president, Jacobo Arbenz Guzman, was a dangerous communist who needed to be overthrown. Another of Bernays' campaigns promoted a cartoon character named Señorita Chiquita Banana.

The only competitor of United Fruit was Standard Fruit and Steamship Company. It sat somewhat below the radar. Owning about a third the number of ships as United's 160, Standard worked together with United rather than as a direct competitor. The same eastern establishment bankers backed both. Standard operated with little publicity, not having the big guns such as the Dulles brothers on their board of directors. To the company's credit, they brought the first jobs, hospitals, schools, and other amenities to the working people in the Central American countries.

Allen Dulles had put together a plan to invade Cuba while John Foster Dulles was Secretary of State under Eisenhower. It was approved by Eisenhower and later approved by the Kennedy brothers. The plan was the Bay of Pigs Invasion. United Fruit provided two of the four ships for the invading 1,400 men. Led by E. Howard Hunt of the CIA, United Fruit helped him obtain money and guns. On April 17, 1961, the Cuban-exile invasion force, known as Brigade 2506, landed at beaches along the Bay of Pigs. The invasion was crushed and the Kennedy administration was humiliated. Some exiles escaped to the sea, while the rest were killed or rounded up and imprisoned by Castro's forces. Almost twelve hundred members of Brigade 2056 surrendered, and more than a hundred were killed. After almost two years of negotiations, Castro released them for $53 million in medical supplies and baby food.

President Kennedy fired Allen Dulles and Charles Cabell, who was deputy director of the CIA. At the time, Cabell's brother was mayor of Dallas, Texas. Kennedy also had the sister of the Dulles brothers fired from the U.S. State Department, where she was a career employee.

There are many conspiracy scenarios around the Bay of Pigs and the Kennedy assassination. One thing was certain, the United Fruit Company based in New Orleans would not survive. On September 24, 1969, the company was bought by a prominent Wall Street tycoon, Eli Black. He merged it with other companies he controlled. For many followers of United Fruit, the story ended when Black's body hit Park Avenue at 100 miles an hour on February 3, 1975. In the morning, Black had gone to his office on the forty-fourth floor in the Pan Am Building, located over Grand Central Station. He smashed a window, threw his brief case from it, then followed it out.

United Fruit was a leading power influencer in Washington in the twentieth century. The fortunes of some of the blue-blooded Boston Brahmins were long intertwined with it from the late nineteenth century. They had the power to have the U.S. government make war, and to negotiate treaties that created the legacy of banana republics.

Ulcher had left his job with United Fruit in 1939 to accept a position with Levingston Shipbuilding Company. It was in Orange that he received a request for help from Peter Bednar's wife, Francisca, concerning her husband's imprisonment. Ulcher immediately went to Edgar Brown, Jr., owner of Levingston. Brown contacted President Roosevelt and requested help to get Bednar released. Roosevelt had appreciated the work that Levingston had done on his pet project, the *Sea Otter II*. Because of Brown's request, it was arranged that Bednar would be paroled to the care of Ulcher in Orange. A home for the Bednar family in Orange was provided in an officers' residential development nicknamed "Navy Town."

Levingston arranged for an office for Bednar, where he was assigned to do research and development. After the war, the FBI gave Bednar a security clearance to work in the shipyard, and he moved his family to a home in the old part of Orange.

But the story doesn't end there. In 1947, the U.S. Justice Department issued deportation proceedings for Bednar and his family to be returned to Germany. On September 8, 1945, Harry S. Truman issued "Proclamation 2655—Removal of Alien Enemies," which required any enemy alien to be repatriated, willingly or not.

At that time, the two largest stockholders in Levingston were Paul Mattingly and Edward Malloy. They contacted their lawyer, George W. Brown, Jr., in Beaumont, Texas, to find out what they could do. George was not related to Edgar Brown, Jr., or to the Brown & Root family. It turned out that the only way to keep Bednar in the United States was to have a bill passed by Congress, and that meant approval by both the House and Senate with President Truman signing it. They arranged for a Washington lawyer, H. S. Groesbeck, to help them. Milton West, congressman from the Fifteenth Congressional District in Brownsville, Texas, sponsored the bill to allow the Bednars to stay in America. Of interest, was the fact that the Justice Department claimed that one of the reasons for wanting to deport the Bednar's was the fact that the oldest son was called a "certified idiot" by a U.S. Public Health Services' physician, making him ineligible for admission into the country. Nicknamed "Happy," Peter, Jr. had Down syndrome. The Justice Department said, "It appears he is a Mongolian-type imbecile and would likely become a charge upon the country." When the Justice Department claimed that Happy Bednar would likely end up as a ward of the state, the owners of the shipyard offered to put up a reasonable bond to assure the government that the afflicted child would never become a charge upon the country. The bill passed Congress, and President Truman approved and signed it on May 19, 1948 (H.R. 1022). The family, including Happy, was given status as permanent immigrants in the United States. Happy spent many years working at a community program for the mentally handicapped in Orange, where the whole town loved him. He was truly happy all the sixty-two years of his life.

When Ulcher died in 1951, Peter Bednar, Sr. became the chief engineer at Levingston. Bednar led the company into the pioneering offshore marine construction world. Only a handful of people in Orange knew the story of the ordeal of the Bednar family. As his son, Willie, related to me, his mother had told him that "secrets of the family should be kept in the family."

In 1949, Edgar Brown, Jr. bought a new DC-3 to be used as his plane. He offered this relatively new twin-engine Beechcraft nine-passenger corporate plane to Levingston at a good price, thinking it would be a great asset for the company in their business. My dad recommended the purchase, knowing the operating cost of the plane. He figured that with all the trips that Levingston executives had to make to and from Houston, Dallas, Oklahoma, New Orleans, New York, and California, the plane would easily pay for itself. Also, it would allow Levingston people to spend more time at home with their families instead of having to stay in hotels on the road. Another big plus was that they could fly customers' executives into Orange to inspect the progress of the work in the shipyard. Orange, Texas, was thirty miles from a small commercial airport. But the Brown family owned a private airport with a dirt runway about three miles from the shipyard. In the 1950's, the interstate four-lane highway had not been built through Texas and Louisiana. The access to and from Orange was by two-lane narrow, dangerous roads. There is no doubt that the plane was a great tool. To make their greatest mark on the world, the culture at Levingston had to continue to learn and grow. Besides personal development, this meant getting out in the world and meeting others. Today, the term is "networking", meeting people and staying in touch with them.

From: Willie "Will" Bednar Mon, 20 Dec 2010 16:54:13 -0500 Subject: Re: FW: Levingston's twin beech
To: pmattingly@msn.com

"Paul, thanks for the story, you amaze me with the info you turn up. Now for a bit more info to add to your Beechcraft tale. In October 1959 while attending A&M I broke both bones in my right leg while playing intramural basketball. I was rushed to the hospital where the Doctors operated and placed a 12-inch steel rod in one of the bones to help it mend. The break was so bad that it was decided that I could not continue in school and needed to go home to Orange. Now guess how I got home? Mr. Malloy sent the Twin Beech to College Station with the two pilots and Dad, to bring me back to home. It was quite a sight: there was Willie in a wheelchair with half my old outfit waiting for the plane to land and all of them thinking Man oh man this Bednar guy must be someone special. While

in Orange I had to have a second operation on the leg but within a few months I was strong enough to take a few hours at Lamar hobbling around on crutches and then went back to A&M that next September. Paul thanks again for the note and the chance to tell my little story."

5

Tugboats and "SPAM" for Russia

The connection of Levingston with General Motors Research and its Diesel Electric Power System, led by the legendary Charles Kettering, was one of the keys to the initial success of the Levingston Shipbuilding Company. The marine diesel division was led by President George Codrington, Cleveland Diesel owned by GM, and the personal project of Charles Kettering. GM had reorganized the company in 1937 as the Cleveland Diesel Engine Division of General Motors. Cleveland engines were widely used by the U.S. Navy in WWII, powering submarines, destroyer escorts, and numerous auxiliaries.

    The head of GM was the legendary Alfred Sloan, who is known today as the co-founder with Kettering of the Memorial Sloan-Kettering Cancer Center. It can be said Kettering was second only to Thomas Edison in contributions to American innovation during this period. Charles F. Kettering was a "screwdriver and pliers" inventor who, even today, continues to impact all aspects of our society. He was a co-holder of more than 140 patents and possessed honorary doctorates from nearly thirty universities. Kettering believed strongly in the combination of hard work, ingenuity, and technology to make the world a better place. In association with the DuPont Chemical Company, he was also responsible for the invention of Freon refrigerant for refrigeration and air conditioning systems. He built a house, Ridgeleigh Terrace, in 1914. It is said that this house was the first in the United States to have electric air conditioning. Freon and air conditioning were great achievements for the people living in the hot southern and western parts of America.

In the 1930's, Charles "Boss Ket" Kettering of General Motors embarked on a program to develop a two-cycle lightweight diesel engine for possible use in automobiles. To cut development time, the faster route was to search for, and purchase, a successful diesel manufacturer. Mr. Kettering, always a step ahead, felt a combination of new GM subsidiary organizations and talent, along with GM capital and existing R&D facilities, would surely produce a winner. He bought the Winton Engine Co., (1938) and made George Codrington the president of the Cleveland Diesel Engine Division of General Motors Corp. Charles Kettering, founder of Delco Electric and head of GM Research, had designed a successful two-cycle diesel engine. From this design came the Cleveland Diesel 278A, two-stroke engines in 1938 for marine applications.

Codrington and Levingston joined forces to design and build the historical ocean rescue U.S. Navy's Auxiliary Tugs.

I remember my father talking about George Codrington as one of the most creative and innovative businessmen he had ever known.

The relationship between Kettering and GM Research with diesel electric propulsion continued when Levingston built the 143-foot oceangoing rescue tugs. Levingston Shipbuilders and General Motors had conceived and built a tug with Levingston's own funds in 1941. Ultimately, eighty-eight were built. The Navy was buying large deep-sea tugs 205 feet long for rescue. When the Navy saw the smaller Levingston tug, they immediately purchased it. The first tug they named the USS *Tuscarora*. She was powered by two GM 12-228A diesel engines (750 hp each) turning twin GE electric generators totaling 1,500 hp. Two-stroke "V" types, they were introduced in 1938 by GM. All engines had mechanically controlled unit injectors (patented in 1934 by General Motors). Spinning an eight-foot bronze propeller on a single shaft at twelve knots offered a 12,000-mile range. This would allow it to keep up with convoys. The tugs had a large tripod-mounted derrick and boom with high-pressure water cannons for fire-fighting.

One obstacle was that Levingston was not approved for direct Navy contracts. In that case, the problem was handled by General Motors being the prime contractor with contract number NOs-82425 and Levingston being the subcontractor. Levingston had a nucleus of personnel trained in working with diesel electric power. Most importantly, GM made sure that Levingston received the needed diesel power systems for the tugs. This relationship with GM proved to be significant after the war as the diesel electric power systems proved important in tugs, and later, offshore oil rigs.

When Levingston couldn't meet the demand for the (ATA) auxiliary ocean rescue tugs, Levingston and General Motors arranged for Gulfport Shipbuilding Co. in Port Arthur, Texas, to build twenty-two of the tugs. Gulfport had a young Rice University engineering graduate, E. W. McCarthy, leading the project. His daughter, Sheila, and son-in-law, Walter Umphrey, have donated to various academic institutions and have been honored for gifts such as Baylor University's Sheila and Walter Umphrey Law Center, the Sheila and Walter Umphrey Bridge at Baylor Stadium, and the Sheila Umphrey Recreational Center on Lamar University's main campus in Beaumont, Texas.

Umphrey is a pioneering lawyer in asbestos litigations and tobacco settlements with state governments. Recently, Umphrey was one of the main lawyers representing NFL players with head injuries. Umphrey told me about his father-in-law, E. W. McCarthy, graduating from Rice University as an honor student in engineering and going to work for Gulfport Shipbuilding during World War II. In 1972, Levingston purchased Gulfport.

No one has ever given the tugs their due. Most of us never knew about their contribution to the war effort until the Robin Williams's film, *Mayday—Tugs of War: Rescues by the Forgotten Tugmen of World War II*. The film, which covers the heroic efforts of tugboat crews that rescued ships attacked by German submarines and planes and provided other services for the Allies in WWII, offered a valuable perspective to that period of history. Men who defied Nazi submarines to rescue seamen of torpedoed merchant ships in the icy waters of the North Atlantic and then towed portable harbors to the beaches of Normandy, describe their ordeals and triumphs in their own words.

Today, one of the Levingston-designed and Gulfport-built ATA tugs launched in 1944 and named the *Comanche*, is located on the waterfront in Bremerton, Washington. The Tacoma-based *Comanche* 202 Foundation owns the boat. She won a Battle Star for action in Okinawa during World War II. The *Comanche* is one of the ships most restored to original condition from World War II. Open to the public, she has made trips to local maritime events like the Olympia Harbor Days 2016 Tugboat Races & Festival in Puget Sound since 1973.

USS ATA-177 circa 1944

The Arctic route was the shortest and most direct route for lend-lease aid to the USSR. The Arctic route shipped some 3,964,000 tons of goods. The Pacific route opened in August 1941, but was affected by the start of hostilities between Japan and the United States. After December 1941, only Soviet ships could be used, and, as Japan and the USSR observed a strict neutrality toward each other, only nonmilitary goods could be transported. (Bernd Martin, *Deutschland und Japan im Zweiten Weltkrieg* [Göttingen: Musterschmidt Verlag, 1969]). Primarily they were Studebaker pickup trucks, "Spam" canned ham and pork, and lined boots for extreme cold weather. It has been said that if it weren't for the support of America, the Russians would be speaking German. The Russians were "fight to the death" against the Germans. It has been speculated that Hitler was determined to take over the lands of the Soviet Union and wipe out the citizens. For comparison, less than 150,000 Americans died in the European Campaign. The Soviet Union had an estimated 197 million population in 1941 and in June of 1946, an estimated 170 million, giving a population loss of 27 million.

During World War II, Russia had Navy crews in Orange, Texas, to take delivery of the Levingston (ATA) 143-foot diesel Electric Ocean tugs when they were completed. The Navy re-designated all the tugs in 1944 as ATA, or Ocean Tugs, Auxiliary. The stories from the people of Orange tell of what it was like socializing with the Russians. In the book, *They Called It the War Effort,* by Louis Fairchild, Lanier Nantz tells a story about a Russian ship captain. Her husband was an officer and part owner of Levingston. One night she and her husband were entertaining at the Grove Dinner Club. The Russian, who was sitting at their table, got up to dance. She noticed he needed another drink, so she ordered one. When he sat down, he said, "Who ordered this drink?" She said, "I did." Then he made her taste it before he would drink it.

There was nervousness about the relations between the two peoples even though we were allies in the war. Before World War II, there had been a propaganda build-up about the evils of communism and Russia. This was despite the fact that America had never fought any kind of war with Russia.

Roosevelt was helping Russia, with Moscow the center of global communism. Many prominent Americans thought that overall atheistic communism would become the greatest menace that ever confronted the Free World. They objected to providing military assistance to a perceived enemy of the United States.

When I researched the ATA tugs and the voyages from America to Russia, I realized how we got the food supplies to Russia. While growing up during the Cold War, we were told the Russian people hated us. It wasn't until I met older Russian men in my business career that I discovered that was a myth. I was nervous about the hatred that I had been told that Russians had for Americans. They had been our main enemy for most of my life. When one Russian businessman was introduced to me, he uttered the word "Spam." I thought this was an insult, and he could see it on my face. He explained how many older Russians loved Americans because of the canned meat product called

Spam. I obviously looked confused. He saw my concern and quickly explained that when they were starving during World War II, the Spam they received from Americans saved their lives. A wartime cartoon in *The New Yorker* shows the docks of Murmansk covered with off-loaded containers and a Soviet official having trouble finding the word "Spam" in the dictionary. Spam was one of the many food items sent to the former Soviet Union by the United States under the Lend-Lease Program.

Soviet leader Nikita Khrushchev, best remembered in the United States for threatening to "bury us," conceded that the Soviets had been in critical condition after German armies overran their best agricultural regions. "Without Spam," he reasoned, "we wouldn't have been able to feed our army." (Bruce Heydt, *Spam Again*, Bruce Heydt, [*America in WWII* [June 2006])

The leading Russian military historian, General Dimitri Volkogonov, revealed during the Gorbachev years that Russia's total losses from 1941 to 1945 were 26.6–27 million dead. Ten million of them were Soviet soldiers, dead or missing. Volkogonov was a Russian historian and general who was head of the Soviet military's psychological warfare department. After researching the secret Soviet archives, he published biographies of Joseph Stalin and Vladimir Lenin, among others.

President Roosevelt committed to supporting Russia when Hitler invaded them. Roosevelt had been friendly with Joe Stalin, dictator of Russia, when, in 1933, Roosevelt gave a letter of recognition renewing diplomatic relations with them.

Paul A. Mattingly Jr.

Four Presidents had refused to recognize Russia because of its record of broken agreements. It is reported that from mid-1941, Roosevelt, under lend-lease programs, started shipping billions of dollars of goods which included the food, trucks, and winter soldier boots that the Russians so badly needed - no doubt critical items for the defeat of the German forces at the battle of Stalingrad in a bitter winter cold. The battle probably saved Russia from German rule. Roosevelt's decision to support Russia to defeat the Germans may have been the most significant decision he made, particularly, when the world was divided in a battle of communism versus capitalism.

6

Levingston's Training Program

Another aspect of wartime activities that influenced the direction and culture of Levingston was its robust training program. At the beginning of the war, Levingston only employed around one hundred twenty workers. Young men were going into the military or going to work for defense contractors. Building and growing a skilled workforce was a challenge. In 1940, more than half of the U.S. population had completed no more than an eighth-grade education. Only 6 percent of men and 4 percent of women had completed four years of college. The solution was to provide an education in reading and writing, followed by welding, painting, pipe fitting, inventory control, and reading drawings and instructions.

One of the key steps forward in educating its workforce was Levingston's pioneering effort with arc welding. The advantages of arc welding were apparent: low cost compared to riveting and speed of application and strength. One worker could do the work of two. Properly welded joints and seams were as strong as the surrounding steel. At the time, trained workers who could arc weld couldn't be found. The shortage of trained workers in the shipyards translated into an even more critical problem: finding and rapidly training a new workforce.

The man for the job was a newly married, recent graduate of LSU named Cecil Beeson. He was bigger than life. Beeson's dream was to be a medical doctor, but he had been sidetracked at LSU playing football. He could not do a premedical program concurrently. He chose football. At Levingston, Beeson's job was to hire workers, educate them about shipyard trades, and keep them happy. Beeson had a keen perception of the value of education, and this would turn out to be a trademark throughout his life.

He brought in several important people who influenced the company, including Betty Duhon. In 1950, while a senior in high school, she was recruited and hired by Beeson. She was an excellent typist and became secretary to Dick Allen, Levingston controller, before he left to become the controller of Schlumberger Global Oilfield Service Company.

Many of the applicants did not have a high school diploma, and many could not read and write. They survived by working on farms or fishing. Beeson created a classroom setting to teach new employees literacy skills. It is said that hundreds of workers at Levingston learned how to read and write through these classes. One of his key legacies was the unofficial policy of Levingston to hire any child of a worker during the summer who was attending college. In 1972, the records show that Levingston hired 150 college students for summer work.

On June 14, 1949, Texas Governor Beauford Jester signed the bill creating the Lamar State College of Technology in

Beaumont, Texas, with a focus on engineering and science. On September 1, 1951, the Texas Legislature promoted the school to a four-year institution. The name was changed to Lamar University in 1971. Beeson became a regent and served for eighteen years, with the last three years as vice chairman of the board. Beeson did such an extraordinary job as a visionary leader that the board of trustees honored him by naming the Cecil Beeson Building on the Lamar campus after him.

In addition to serving as the head of personnel training, Beeson was the safety director. Shipyard work is among the most hazardous of occupations, and Beeson ran a highly-regarded safety program. He constantly pushed for equipment to make the work environment safer. Among the workforce were workers with relatives and good friends on staff, so the emphasis on safety was exceptionally high. Levingston had a reputation as one of the safest shipyards around. This proved to be an asset in recruiting Gulf Coast workers.

Beeson also established a mentor program for experienced, skilled workers to train the rookies. He worked with the local high schools to send workers for education. Beeson treated the workers as if he were their counselor and doctor. If they had personal problems, they knew they could ask him for help. The management of Levingston appreciated his skills and gave him full rein in his educational projects. The result was a skilled workforce that was considered one of the best of any Gulf Coast shipyard.

It is obvious that Levingston was very good at focusing on customers and the marketplace. This didn't just happen.

They aggressively worked at it. The potential customers were limited, and the key to success was getting repeat business. Even though Levingston was unionized, Brown & Root Construction, an anti-union company, used Levingston for building their derrick and pipe-laying barges and for the repairs because, as one former employee of Brown & Root stated, "They are the best."

7

The Cajuns Come to Orange

World War II served as a milestone event in the migration of industrial workers to the upper Texas Gulf Coast. War-related petrochemical plants and shipyards drove the westward migration of French-speaking Cajuns across the Sabine River, the natural border that separates Louisiana from Texas. Companies like Levingston Shipbuilding provided Cajuns with skills and technical training that did not exist in Louisiana, and which many later applied to extended careers in shipbuilding and the offshore oil and gas industry.

Cajuns are known to be entrepreneurs in their ability to survive. To this day, it is still possible to live off hunting, frogging, trapping, shrimping, harvesting crawdads, and fishing in the Cajun area of South Louisiana called Acadiana. It comprises twenty-two parishes plus the Texas counties of Orange and Jefferson on the West to the Mississippi River on the East. To the south is the Gulf of Mexico. Acadiana is a designation recognizing the Cajun culture.

In *They Called It the War Effort*, historian Louis Fairchild examined the ordinary lives of citizens and shipyard workers, including the Cajuns. Wartime production in Orange was a story of "adjustment and the remarkable transformation of a sleepy little southern town into a vigorous wartime shipbuilding center," Fairchild wrote. Orange experienced the typical boomtown sensation. With the huge expansion in shipyards, the city leaders struggled to find and build ample housing and facilities to support the thousands of workers and their families. As America's involvement in a two-front war expanded in 1942, Orange built more family housing and dormitories for female workers. By 1943, the city added ten thousand more housing units, four cinemas, and three elementary schools. With wartime, governmental rationing of gasoline and tires, the residents of Orange typically walked to work, the grocery store, or local restaurants.

Beginning in 1942, buses shuttled teams of recruiters over the Sabine River to seek workers in South Louisiana. These recruiters also hired workers from Dallas, parts of East Texas, and as far away as Alabama and Kentucky. Many Cajuns from across the Sabine joined the ranks. Per Fairchild, by 1945, the population in Orange surged to sixty thousand, about a 700 percent increase from 1940.

During the Texas, Golden Triangle's wartime boom, Cajun shipbuilders made up a large segment of the population. A large number could not speak English. As one participant in Fairchild's oral history project explained, "We'd hire a whole group of French people and only one or two of 'em could speak English…We'd take one person that could speak English and give him extra training, and he'd be the supervisor for that group." Nevertheless, they had basic knowledge and common sense, and they knew how to work with their hands. In the shipyards like Levingston, they learned how to use measurements and read blueprints and learned fundamental mechanical skills. The repetitious assembly-line mass-production techniques helped facilitate the learning curve and fostered these skills. Factory work also taught the Cajuns professionalism and skills in working with culturally diverse colleagues in a complex industrial work environment.

One notable Cajun who migrated to the Golden Triangle, went not for work in the shipyards, but to make his mark in the entertainment field. He was Cajun swing innovator, Leo Soileau, who performed with his Rhythm Boys. He commented that the shipyard workers were good customers, tipped well, danced a lot, and requested a variety of songs, from Western swing tunes such as "San Antonio Rose" to the French waltz "Big Mamou." This Cajun band performed several new Western tunes made popular by Bob Wills, Gene Autry, and Hank Williams. They also played Cajun swing favorites such as "Grand Texas," "Austin Special," and "Port Arthur Blues" as well as the big band sounds of Glenn Miller,

After the war, many Cajun shipyard workers remained in the Golden Triangle area and established French-speaking communities of their own. Gradually, these "Texas Cajuns" moved on to Houston and other parts of Texas, but it was the pull of wartime work at the shipyards in and around Orange that initially attracted many native-born Cajuns to settle west of the Sabine River. Through their unique cultural traits of music, cuisine, and celebrated lifestyle, the *joie de vivre* of "Texas Cajuns" has added a cultural ambiance to Southeast Texas that is still evident three quarters of a century later.

Together with other folks from East Texas and academically trained engineers from abroad, the Cajun workforce established a core competence and expertise in shipbuilding at

Levingston during the 1940's, even though many of them had little or no education. When the war ended and the company transitioned into the offshore rig construction market, it inherited the skilled expertise and extensive knowledge from this core group of wartime ship fitters that ultimately built Levingston into a great company that did great things.

In a sense, Levingston became more of a Louisiana Cajun company than a Texas company. Cajun surnames like Thibodeaux, Broussard, LeBlanc, Duhon, Breaux, Cormier, Hebert, Fontenot, and Prejean, to name a small sampling, belonged to people reared on farms or in the coastal marshes of South Louisiana. They became synonymous with the Levingston culture and that of Orange and the surrounding areas of Southeast Texas.

"There were several of them [Cajuns] who could not read or write," said Larry Baker, Sr., a Levingston pioneer, "but they could do you one heck of a job, because that's what they did on the farm, with the rice and the sugarcane." The Cajun people had no formal education, but were forced to build things and repair things on the farms or out in the marshes or on boats using only their hands and ingenuity and some trial and error.

They used the same technique, with some basic on-the-job training, to be ship fitters and machinists and welders. And as the word spread, Levingston sought relatives of these workers who had developed a similar work ethic on the small-town farms and in the coastal hamlets. It wasn't long before Cajuns outnumbered all other ethnic groups, including local Texans, working at Levingston.

The word *Cajun* commands a lot of respect in the marine offshore oil industry. In 1953, the movie *Thunder Bay*, starring iconic movie actor, James Stewart, featured the Louisiana shrimping industry and the offshore oil business. Shrimpers and oilmen clash when an ambitious wildcatter begins constructing an offshore oil rig. It has a successful conclusion with the shrimpers and the oil men learning to live together. Levingston executives were a small part of the financial backers of the movie.

The Cajun humor was a big part of life at Levingston shipyard. They brought a community of workers together who prized laughter, joy, and singing with hard work and exceptional performance. The Cajuns' celebrations of communal harvests, community cookouts, and neighborhood dances frequently brought in extended family members to join in with the shipyard workers. Many of these company-family events occurred at the Levingston Employees Recreation Association (LERA), a forty-acre park owned by Levingston for providing a place for their employees to have barbeques, shrimp and crawfish boils, and Easter egg hunts.

Working as a team was natural for Cajuns, and they carried it into the shipyard. One of the sayings in Orange was that there were two types of people who came out of Louisiana: preachers and storytellers. A common saying among the Cajuns was, "For God's sake, be a storyteller. The world's got too many preachers." The shipyard was full of storytellers and crafty Cajuns from the bayous. For example, Milton Leger, a native of Crowley, Louisiana, moved to Orange in the late 1940's and trained and worked at Levingston as a welder. He also played the fiddle as a professional musician for many years with the Starburst Boys Band at dance halls and radio stations all over the Gulf South.

The Cajuns also adopted their own brand of dark coffee which they brought into the shipyard. Throughout the Levingston premises, there were percolators that continually brewed a 100 percent dark-roast coffee that carried the brand name of "Seaport," produced by the Texas Coffee Company in Beaumont, Texas. It has a bold and strongly rich flavor that has been described as "true Cajun coffee." Some Texans refer to it as "true Texas style." Texas Coffee Company was founded in Beaumont in 1921 by Charles J. Fertitta, Sr., who later included R. C. Maceo and Joseph Serio in the business. Their ancestors were some of the first Sicilians to immigrate to the United States through New Orleans. One member of the family describes their lineage as the "first family" in the Sicilian world, not unlike the English families who came to America on the *Mayflower.*

Seaport is still made by the Texas Coffee Company and owned and run by the fourth generation of family members. Across the Sabine River from Texas in Louisiana, Seaport Coffee runs directly in competition with Baton Rouge–based Community Coffee, which also claims to be the "true Cajun coffee. Shipyard workers called their Seaport "real coffee, something to wake you up," and added comments like, "not that weak brown water you get from most coffees." It was like a badge of acceptance to drink Seaport. Real men drank it black, with no cream or sugar, sipping it slowly like fine wine.

The practice of having coffee available in shipyards all day long started during World War II. It was thought that coffee would boost cognitive abilities. Sometime after the war, it became popular to eat donuts with one's coffee. Equipment and material supply salesmen would join in the coffee breaks, bringing in the donuts. This provided a time for the workers to learn about new products, discuss work-related problems with the salesmen, and seek knowledge and ingenuity in helping to solve them.

Where did the Cajuns come from? In the 1600's a group of French people left Europe for the Canadian province called Acadia, now known as Nova Scotia. It was along the coast on the Bay of Fundy that the first French settlers to come to the New World arrived in 1605, before any had arrived from England. They prospered by doing things like draining the swamps of the Bay of Fundy tidelands and building dikes and canals, and converting the useless swamps into fertile farmland. To do this, they forged a unique bond of a strong communal effort. This community effort is still in place in South Louisiana more than two hundred years later. It was that skill that set the Acadians apart from the other French settlers who soon followed and populated Quebec.

British control of the Acadia colony began in 1710. By 1755, the British decided to kick out all Acadians from Acadia. It was a form of British genocide to destroy the Acadian culture. The deportations took place over several years. Thousands of Acadians had their possessions confiscated, their homes and farms burned. Many died in transportation as the British scattered them to America and to France and different parts of the world. The Spanish controlled Louisiana and took in some of the Acadians. Later, thousands who had been sent back to France would immigrate to Louisiana.

Cajun influence at Levingston also spread to Singapore. In 1981, John H. Huff was President of Western Oceanic when he negotiated a deal with Keppel FELS to build a $100 million semisubmersible drilling rig. It was a landmark project because of its large size. Huff recalls, "They celebrated [the deal] with a Cajun-style crawfish boil." The Keppel FELS executives bought a case of Dom Perignon. This was something new for the Texas and Louisiana crew, washing down crawfish with a glass of high-dollar champagne!

Berdon Lawrence, of Lake Charles, Louisiana, who started in the towing and barge business in the early 1960's, told me that in the pioneering days, all the tugboat captains were Cajuns. They had started out working on shrimp boats. They were excellent at what they did. He noticed that many of them had young deckhands close by. When he inquired about this, he found out that the captains were illiterate, and they used the young deckhands to read for them and fill out the logs. Lawrence said the Cajuns were the best of the best in the profession of tugboat captaining.

He later merged his company into Kirby Corporation and became chairman of the board. Headquartered in Houston, Texas, it is the largest tank barge operator in the United States, transporting bulk liquid products throughout the Mississippi River System, on the Gulf Intracoastal Waterway, along all three U.S. coasts, and in Alaska and Hawaii. Kirby's market cap in 2014 was $5.1 billion.

Levingston shipbuilders were known for their colorful nicknames, such as *Frenchie*. It was a way of being part of the group. If you were given a nickname, this meant you were accepted. With all the characters from many different places, the need for creating bonding was necessary. Names like *Shorty, Bulldog,*

Rebel, Horse Face, Stinky, Snake, High Pockets, Chicken Man, and *Shifty* were created. One nickname or slang word commonly used around the shipyard was *Sumbeech,* —southern for "son of a bitch." It was used for everything: a new product, modifications, pieces of equipment, and even people.

A characteristic of the Levingston work environment was the playfulness among the crew. While they worked, it was not unusual to tell jokes and play pranks on each other. Ed Malloy had an office that resembled a bar, complete with paintings of dogs playing cards and a brass spittoon in the corner of the office. It gave the feeling that working in a shipyard was supposed to be fun.

The shipyard culture at Levingston was unique, in part because of the Cajun influence that created a laid-back working atmosphere. But they also got the job done and had respect for each other and for the leaders of the company. And the leaders ran the company as if the employees were one big extended family. This closeness created a bond that held the entire community together. Ideas are easy; executing those ideas with a well-led team is paramount. The work of the Levingston leaders was inclusive, aware, and attuned to the needs of their workers and customers.

Larry Baker, Sr. summed up the character of the Levingston shipyard workers throughout the early postwar era of offshore marine construction, "We were blessed with good, hardworking people who wanted to do a good job," he said. "And they were proud of their work. Some of them wore their hard hats, their badges, and their steel-toe boots to get married!"

8

Talent

To grow, Levingston needed to hire. One of their brilliant moves was the bringing on board of a young engineer, Mr. Otho Haunschild from Missouri. He had come to Texas working for a railroad company. After World War II, Haunschild became the general superintendent who proved to be a top-notch builder and who rose to be president of Levingston. Haunschild's daughter, Ann, married John Bookout, Jr. whose father was the legendary president of Shell Oil Co. John, Jr. is active today in the oil business as a consultant and a director of the McDermott Company.

Robert "Sonny" Fogal, Jr. retired after over fifty-seven years in oil and gas as one of the icons in the offshore industry. He did front-line work as Zentech's Director of Business Development. Zentech's president, Ramesh Maini, noted on August 28, 2014, "All the serious players in our industry know Bob and his many accomplishments. He is clearly among the elite in this group."

Fogal started his career in the 1950's at Levingston Shipbuilding Company where his father worked and earlier, his grandfather had, as well. Fogal and fellow Levingston employee, Don Covington, married twin sisters. Both Fogal and Covington have sons working in the shipbuilding industry.

John Reid was a black man who started at Levingston during World War II. Reid was in jail for life for the murder of a man. His wife, Corrine, worked in the home of my parents and the home of Ed Malloy, as well. Corinne asked them if they would try to get him out of jail. When they looked into the case, they found that he had indeed killed a man, but it was a case of self-defense. They got him out on parole, and he went to work at the shipyard. John was a big, powerful man who became a leader of the black workers in the shipyard. Ed Malloy and my dad started using John to chauffeur clients around, and later he became Malloy's personal chauffeur. He also worked as the head bartender at the christening parties in Levingston's private facility, the Bilge Club.

Clarence Levingston was a member of the founding Levingston family who had started the company in 1859. Clarence was a key leader in the engineering department, starting his career there during World War II. He was a graduate of Rice University (Rice Institute at the time) in Houston, Texas.

Frank Malloy was the younger brother of Ed Malloy, who came to Levingston in 1941. Frank was a good salesman whose main client was Humble Oil. Humble is pronounced "Um-bull." The "h" is silent. His wife, Colette, was an elegant lady who was extremely helpful in entertaining. Neither Frank nor his brother had any children. When Colette died in 1963, Frank married her sister, Imelda Jane Curran, whose husband, Vernon Skinner, had died in 1951 in front of her, her two sons, Sam and David, and Frank Malloy. The two sons later inherited the Malloy estate. Sam became a celebrity when President George H. W. Bush appointed him as Secretary of Transportation from 1989 to 1991 and then as White House Chief of Staff, succeeded by James A. Baker III.

Skinner's wife became a close friend of President Bush's daughter, Doro Bush Koch. Sam's brother, David, worked for Levingston in the 1960's until the early 1970's when he went into the stock brokerage business in Beaumont. David was the stockbroker in the sale of Levingston to Ashland Oil. Sam Skinner is known to be well-liked, and the fact that President Bush had worked with his uncle/stepfather at Levingston Shipbuilding in his pioneering days while CEO at Zapata, did not hurt. Sam Skinner's daughter, Jane Skinner Goodell, a former daytime news anchor who worked for Fox News, is married to Roger Goodell, the Commissioner of the National Football League.

The story of Levingston requires an accounting of the role of Price Waterhouse and Co. (now known as PricewaterhouseCoopers). Edgar Brown, a major investor in Levingston, was a believer in a good control mechanism to know what the costs are and where your money will make a profit. His good friend, Harry Weiss, was one of the original founders of Humble Oil & Refining Company (ExxonMobil). Weiss talked Edgar Brown into going to Price Waterhouse and Co.

(PW), an accounting firm which had opened a Houston, Texas, branch office in the late 1930's.

The CPA firm's major client was the John D. Rockefeller family and their business holdings. Legend in Beaumont has it that the original papers for the formation of Humble Oil (1911) were signed at Weiss's home in Beaumont located at the corner of Fifth and McFadden. At the time, Weiss was twenty-four years old. The home is still there.

Jesse H. Jones, Houston banker, bought 25 percent of Humble's stock under the condition that the company move to Houston and locate in one of his office buildings. Standard Oil of New Jersey bought 50 percent of Humble Oil in 1919. It wasn't until 1959 that Humble was merged with Standard Oil of New Jersey, the new name of which became Exxon in 1973. Weiss served as president of Humble from 1937 to 1948. Today, the Houston Museum of Natural Science's Weiss Energy Hall, named after Harry Weiss, is one of the most outstanding exhibits about the oil industry in the world.

Weiss had encouraged Edgar W. Brown, Jr. to attend Princeton University where Weiss had received an engineering degree. The Weiss family and the Brown family had been close friends for decades, and both families were pioneers in the lumber business. Weiss was a major contributor to Rice University and his former home in Houston is now the residence of the school's President.

My father, Paul A. Mattingly, Sr., CPA, was handling the Edgar Brown account at Price Waterhouse & Co., when Brown talked my father into quitting and moving to Orange and working for him. He let my father bring his assistant at PW, R. R. "(Dick") Allen, with him. Later, Allen became controller for Schlumberger Limited, where he retired in the 1970's when Schlumberger moved their corporate offices from Houston to New York. Years later, they moved back to Houston. Allen told me the most fun he ever had working was when he lived in Orange and was employed at Levingston.

During World War II, another PW CPA named Malcolm Vaughan, who later became president of Levingston and co-owner of Baker Marine, came on board. By the end of World War II, Levingston had three CPAs working for them. My father also got Walter Pennington, timekeeper, to come into the accounting department. Pennington later became president of Levingston. He died in the late 1960's, at the peak of the glory days at the shipyard. After the war, my father hired Virginia Baker, who became the financial manager for Far East Levingston Shipbuilding in Singapore and controller for Baker Marine, Inc.

Another associate of my father at Price Waterhouse was Lamar Muse, who later did the audits on Levingston for PW. Muse and my father had a common hobby: they both played the clarinet. Lamar Muse left in 1948 to help start up Trans Texas Airways and later became the first president of Southwest Airlines. Muse put in a profit-sharing plan at Southwest that is still in place today. It is the same profit-sharing plan that was implemented at Levingston Shipbuilding, and also at Marine & Petroleum Supply Company, an affiliated company that my father bought when he left Levingston in 1952. Basically, the company takes a percent of taxable income and distributes it to all employees in cash and/or company stock. The concept is simply to encourage employees to act as part owners of the business.

Southwest is recognized as the most successful and innovative company in the history of the global airline industry. In the year 2015, Southwest Airlines paid $620 million in profit-sharing to employees. The amount was as much as two month's pay for some employees. Not bad for a U.S. domestic airline.

Larry Lamping, my godfather, was another associate of the Levingston group of Price Waterhouse CPAs. Lamping oversaw the Price Waterhouse team that audited Southwest Airlines from the beginning. Lamping was a pallbearer at Muse's funeral.

Cost control was fundamental to the survival of a shipbuilding firm like Levingston. Also, to be successful, one had to know the basics: the terminology of the shipbuilding industry and what each worker did, and then stay heavily engaged in cost and time-saving changes. The accounting department was intentionally situated in the middle of the shipyard. You could walk out your office door and go a few feet to the work being done. After World War II, my father became part owner of Levingston Shipbuilding Company with Ed Malloy, and they closely integrated the accounting system and shipyard work. By doing this, the leaders at Levingston had immediate data on the daily progress of costs and product delivery schedules.

Unfortunately, rig building was based on adversarial relationships. Owners, contractors, subcontractors' suppliers, all are trying to get the best price—the ultimate customer being the one who will pay for the rig from his drilling operation. This put pressure on everyone to keep the costs down. The pressure point was at the shipyard. The sophisticated cost accounting system installed at Levingston gave them a significant competitive advantage over competing shipyards in managing construction costs. The goal was a job under budget within the time schedule, meeting tight quality specifications. It demanded relationships that benefited all parties. The concept was to promote team spirit, not only with employees but with all the businesses involved.

In the accounting department, Levingston had an extraordinary young man, Walter (Penny) E. Pennington, who had started at the shipyard as a timekeeper. Penny knew all the marine terminology and the jobs involved to do the work. He was the key to identifying the work, describing it clearly, and creating a fantastic cost accounting system. My father described Penny as a man who knew everything about shipbuilding. He knew the terminology and how much labor it took to do the work. When Levingston created an invoice for their work, Penny would write the invoice describing in detail the work performed. A local from Orange, he had an even temperament and the advantage of a brilliant wife, Ollie, who also worked in the shipyard as executive assistant to the president, Ed Malloy. Penny had a younger brother, Vernon, who headed up the electrical department. He was employed at Levingston until his retirement.

The story of the Pennington family and their reputation for "integrity" was a key characteristic of the Levingston culture. Culture is established through leadership, starting in the family. From there it moves out into the world of schools, businesses, and governments. Penny later proved to be an outstanding president of Levingston and a leader in their unique business culture development. Unfortunately, he died of a heart attack in 1967 in the middle of the "1960's glory days."

Ollie was a very nice and smart lady who was good at judging people. The Pennington's had no children and Levingston Shipbuilding Company filled a huge part of their lives. Both were natives of Orange, Texas. Ollie's maiden name was Gomez. Her family had emigrated from Barcelona, Spain. The Gomez family owned and operated a restaurant at the Holland Hotel in downtown Orange. Ollie's sister, Hazel, married John Daugherty, Sr., a Houstonian who became a prominent oilfield executive with Mid Continent Supply Co., the flagship of nineteen companies under the Ken Davis Industries umbrella. All the companies were in the oilfield service business.

Daugherty had worked with Ken Davis when Davis bought a chain of small oilfield supply stores. Davis was a brilliant, but tough, leader who was given the oilfield nickname of "Stinky" because of his toughness. The nineteen companies rose to become major leaders among the oilfield services companies of the world. They owned the largest drilling contractor, Loffland Bros. Daugherty, one of the most respected men in the oil business, had a stroke, and then Davis died in 1968.

Years later, when the oil companies ended up in a downswing, Davis' companies eventually ended up in bankruptcy.

Daugherty's son chose not to follow his dad in the oil business, but rather to go into residential real estate. In 1967, John Daugherty founded John Daugherty Realtors in Houston. It is recognized as the number one real estate firm for luxury homes in River Oaks, Tanglewood, Memorial, West University Place and other Houston neighborhoods.

If there is one word to describe John Daugherty and his business, it is "integrity." This is the same word that was used to describe the lives of his aunt and uncle, Walter and Ollie Pennington, in Orange, Texas, and his parents, John and Hazel Daugherty, in Houston.

John tells the story of the establishment of his real estate business in Houston. One of his older mentors, Chester Grubbs from Orange, Texas, a childhood friend of his mother, arranged for an office and a deposit for a telephone in one of Grubb's buildings on Waugh Drive in Houston. This enabled Daugherty to start his business.

Walter "Penny" Pennington was raised as a member of the First Baptist Church of Orange. But he was so impressed with his wife, Ollie's, spirituality that he converted to Catholicism. In later years, she attended the predominately African American Catholic Church, St. Theresa's, where she was more comfortable.

At Levingston, Ollie was a leader in working to get fair treatment for African American employees. During this period, it is significant to know that Orange had an active

KKK membership and segregation was a strong part of the American culture. It was a battle for blacks to get recognition. I know for fact that people like my father, Ed Malloy, and Walter Pennington worked with dedication in seeing that the black workers at the shipyard were fairly treated.

The Gomez restaurant at the old Holland Hotel in Orange was well- known as an up-scale restaurant. The Holland Hotel opened in 1902 and was recognized as one of the finest hotels in the South.

Orange was a center of the lumber business, and timber barons traveled to Orange to do business. At the time, the mayor of Orange was J. W. Link, a wealthy lawyer and timber man who dreamed of building a great city. Link built one of the biggest mansions in the South on Green Avenue, and was one of the backers of the hotel. A few years later, he decided to move to Houston and create a major residential development called Montrose, building Montrose Boulevard down the middle. The centerpiece of the development was his mansion, the largest home in Houston, which is now the administration building of the University of St. Thomas. It is known as the Link-Lee Mansion. The name Lee comes from the family that purchased the home from Link in 1916. T. P. Lee was a wealthy banker who funded the famous wildcatter, Frank Yount of Beaumont, creating the Yount-Lee oil company. Another major stockholder in the company was grocery man, John Henry Phelan. The company was sold in the middle of the 1930's depression to Amoco for one of the largest cash transactions for a company, at the time, ever recorded in America.

John (Don) Hoffpauir as a true German who was a living legend for designing and fixing marine mechanical stuff. He had several patents, such as ones for internal combustion engine overload and coupling and steering apparatus for a single screw tug. Don did not have an engineering degree, but he had the ability to conceive problem-solving solutions and how to make them work. Hoffpauir, as a young man in Louisiana at the age of twenty-one, was put in charge of running a rice mill. He had to learn about mechanics, hydraulics, and electricity to keep the machinery running. He was a machinist and could figure out how to make things. One can't say enough about the significance of having such a talent. It is like a football team with a "super-star" quarterback. Yet Hoffpauir has not been recognized in historical records. He was quiet, and, of course, Levingston's worst nightmare was to lose him to a competitor. My father told me that Don was the smartest man he knew in shipbuilding. Numerous others who worked with him said the same thing. It was reported that at one time Hoffpauir was the highest paid employee of Levingston. Hoffpauir was soft-spoken and easy to get along with. He was a team player. Anybody could go to him with a problem, and he would help solve it. He was the key man in developing the Levingston class of independent leg jack-ups. In 2013, Noble Drilling had eight Levingston class jack-up rigs still working in their fleet. Hoffpauir developed a unique method of retching up and down the legs on jack-up rigs. They worked closely with Armco, who manufactured the legs. This technology gave Levingston the edge they needed to gain a major foothold in the offshore jack-up rig business. Don died in 1974, at age sixty-one.

My father, Paul Mattingly, grew up in a small farming community, Chaffee, Missouri, near Cape Girardeau. His parents were divorced, and he had to work his way through Saint Louis University as a janitor at the school. He was proud of having worked his way through college and was grateful to the Jesuit priests for allowing him to get a college education. My father always preached simplicity. From engineering to accounting to operations, the theme at Levingston was simplification.

The culture at Levingston was based on strong leadership, but was benevolent to all associates. Rather than rule by committee, they made decisions by teams of individuals. The stress at the top was intense. The big concerns they constantly had to deal with were making promised delivery dates and controlling costs.

My father sold his interest in Levingston in 1954. He then bought his partners out in Marine & Petroleum Supply Company, which the owners of Levingston had founded in 1946. We moved to Houston, where he started a small industrial park on the west side of the city off the Old Katy Freeway. My brothers and I still own the park. When my father died in 1975, my six brothers, widowed mother, and employees took over the running of the business. We redirected it from a marine supplier to a gasket-and-sealing business, catering to the chemical, refining, and oilfield manufacturing businesses. It was sold to Coltec Industries in 1999. Since then, we have bought back three of the six divisions that we owned and operated. The most important thing we learned from our father was the "can-do" spirit that he had helped create at Levingston. He was both result-oriented and always eager to get on to the next task. Levingston taught him to be flexible in experimentation and to learn from making mistakes.

9
Lake Maracaibo, Venezuela

The challenge in an organization such as Levingston is getting things done in a world of imperfect people and ambiguous choices. We look to leadership. We see all kinds of literature and work sessions on this topic. It becomes scary with all the complex theories and rhetoric about what it takes. Leadership is like playing baseball or the piano, or speaking a foreign language. It takes skills that can be learned and mastered with practice. In a sense, the folks at Levingston were mavericks in the leadership field.

In the early 1950's, Levingston was a pioneer in Venezuela. They had built seven ferryboats that crossed Lake Maracaibo from the city of Maracaibo to Caracas. The famous New York naval architect, Eads Johnson, designed them. The *Cacique*, a 159-foot steel, double-end diesel ferryboat built for the Venezuelan Company, La Translacustre, was christened in Orange by my mother, Maureen Kelly Mattingly. She was greatly honored to have been chosen by La Translacustre.

Her mother, Mary Kelly, and sister, Susie Kelly, traveled by train from St. Louis, Missouri, for the grand event.

Levingston established a shipyard in Maracaibo with Venezuelan partners in the 1950's. The partners were the same people who owned the ferryboat company, La Translacustre. They were members of the Samuel Belloso banking and business empire.

Lake Maracaibo is a vast body of water where tremendous oil and gas reserves were discovered early in the twentieth century. Before the construction of a bridge across the lake in the 1950's, the city of Maracaibo was isolated from the rest of Venezuela, and the only way in or out of the city was by boat. Levingston built a diesel electric ferry for operation on Lake Maracaibo, and after the war, the company built an additional six ferryboats for Lake Maracaibo. Levingston agreed to become partners with John Shortt, president of the ferryboat companies that owned the seven diesel electric ferryboats Levingston had built.

Maureen Mattingly (my mother) christening the *Cacique* Venezuelan ferry.

Shortt's wife, Hortensia, was a Belloso, a wealthy and powerful family in Venezuela. They were in banking, ranching, ownership of the ferryboat company, distribution of wholesale drugs in Venezuela, and in a joint venture with a major U.S. pharmaceutical manufacturer. The people at Levingston had the expertise and contacts and were excited thinking of the prospect of a shipyard in Lake Maracaibo. But even back in the 1950's, the political situation in Venezuela was unstable. As it turned out, it became more unstable. One of the big hurdles was hiring and training people to do the work. For the few Venezuelans, you had to compete with the oil companies. Finally, after about ten years, the Shortt family decided to liquidate the company. They were being harassed by the government over the shipyard and with their other business interests, they didn't need the frustration. Most customers in Venezuela just bought the marine equipment in the United States from Levingston and transported it to Venezuela. The experience in the Maracaibo shipyard proved to the people at Levingston that they had the knowledge and the ability to start up a shipyard in another country. The opportunity came a few years later in Singapore.

Shortt and Levingston also founded a tug and barge company in 1957 called Zulia Towing and Barge Company to work in the Lake Maracaibo area. Shortt later bought Levingston's interest in the company. The company was nationalized in 2009 by the Venezuelan government.

10

New York Harbor

New York Harbor is well known for its tugboats. Tugboats have been operating there since at least the early 1800's. The first known tugboat was invented in New York Harbor in 1828 with the conversion of an old steam side paddle wheeler, the *Rufus W. King*, to a towboat. No name is more clearly identified with the tugboat business than Moran Towing Corporation. The company owns and operates ninety-five tugs and barges that service sixteen ports. Moran Towing traces its origins to 1850, when Michael Moran, a twenty-two-year-old immigrant from Ireland, landed in New York aboard one of the hundreds of so-called "coffin ships" that evacuated more than a million starving refugees from Ireland during the Great Famine of 1845–52. Moran made money as a mule driver on the Erie Canal, using money he had saved to buy a barge. A century later, Moran Towing grew to become one of the leading tugboat companies in America, with a huge presence in New York Harbor and the surrounding area. He prospered and established himself through a towing operation. Upon finding a couple of his subordinates drunk and fighting, he would seize them and start banging their heads together, meanwhile crying out admonitions mixed with Scripture.

In 1948, Moran Towing contracted with Levingston shipyard to build five steel-hulled, diesel-electric, 106-foot-long tugs. Per *The New York Times*, Moran wanted to "ensure the most modern harbor fleet in the world for the postwar period." These boats were powered by a single diesel-electric General Motors Cleveland 16-278A engine, single screw, rated at 1,750 horsepower. There were magazine articles, paintings by marine artists, photographs, and books celebrating the five new Levingston-built Grace-class tugs, all named after Moran family members: Barbara, Carol, Doris, Grace, and Moira Moran.

A million-dollar order by a relatively small, privately owned tugboat company was a show of confidence in the ability of the American capitalist system to respond to the challenge of creating postwar jobs. It was a great show of being "bullish on America." The world needed "animal spirits" for the job of gaining confidence and rebuilding what was lost during the war. There were many predictions that unless major government intervention was brought to bear, the end of World War II would produce unemployment and industrial dislocation. The economist Paul Samuelson, a future Nobel Prize winner, predicted in 1943 that upon cessation of hostilities and demobilization, millions of men would be thrown out of the labor force. He warned that unless wartime controls were extended, America could face another economic depression. However, those predictions of doom did not happen. In the first few years after World War II, the nation entered a period of great prosperity. By the end of the war, the federal government accounted for 55 percent of the domestic product, dropping to 17 percent by 1947.

New York City was the largest city in the world and a leading industrial manufacturing center, thanks in part to its port facilities and one of the biggest harbors in the world. Most of the large port cities in Europe suffered major damage in WWII. Tokyo was burnt to a crisp from firebombing. New York was set for a major postwar economic boom.

In April 1948, the tugboat *Grace Moran*, the first such Moran tug built by Levingston, was accorded an all-out welcome to New York City as she cruised in on her maiden voyage from Orange. The Grace class was designed by noted tug designer, Joe Hack. The General Motors diesel-electric systems offered much more precise maneuverability and quick throttle response, which is vital in an environment in which a wrong move could overturn a tug or crush it between a ship and a dock.

Two years later, the fleet of five tugs, the last of which was completed in Orange in 1949, made a convincing performance when they docked the *Queen Mary*, the world's second-largest luxury liner. Moran docked the vessel with the five Grace-class, diesel-electric tugs instead of ten miscellaneous crafts, as formerly required to dock the *Queen Mary* and her larger sister, the *Queen Elizabeth*. These two liners were considered the finest luxury liners in the world and were used to ship tens of thousands of returning GIs home from overseas duty. The fanfare of the five tugs at a cost of a million dollars was publicized in the news media as the work of a little tugboat company believing in America. Levingston built an additional four diesel-electric tugs for Tracy Towing Line to also operate in New York Harbor. John Caddell, whose family founded the Caddell Company in New York in 1903 and operated several drydocks there, recalled the Levingston-built tugs: *"I am always awed by their heavy but beautiful construction and, especially, with the new GM16-278 diesel-electric engines that powered them. The electric power plants allowed the tugs to maneuver at a very, very slow speed, thus allowing the captains better control of their tows when in tight quarters. They were rated at 1600 horsepower, but even then, with all that power, the tugs could put barges to the pier without breaking an eggshell…that was good for us not to damage our piers, but the other side of the coin was that they didn't damage their barges either, giving us less work! They were beautiful tugs and were finally sold when Tracy went out of business. Towing coal barges around New York, however, was hard on the electric propulsion motors, as coal dust would find its way into the windings quickly, and I do recall, thus, the tugs were often on down time, repairing and cleaning the motors."*

11

The *John F. Kennedy*

In keeping with the tradition of its diversification, Levingston accepted contracts to build several ferryboats for New York Harbor. The most well-known of these vessels is the *John F. Kennedy*, built by Levingston in the 1960's, and still shuttling passengers and tourists between Manhattan and Staten Island. The current fleet of ferries makes 110 five-mile trips daily. They enjoy a unique place in American history.

On May 27, 1794, "The Commodore," Cornelius Vanderbilt, was born on Staten Island. He began his vast fortune and transportation enterprise by purchasing a boat and establishing ferry service to Manhattan. Since 1905, the City Of New York has owned and operated the Staten Island Ferries.

In 1965, Levingston built the *John F. Kennedy* for the city of New York in honor of President John F. Kennedy, who was assassinated in 1963. Shortly after Kennedy's death, at the christening of the *John F. Kennedy* held at Levingston Shipyard, Robert Kennedy authorized Leo Brown, Commissioner of the Department of Marine and Aviation of the City of New York, to represent the Kennedy family at the nautical tradition of christening and naming ceremony. Mrs. Walter B. Coleman, wife of the deputy commissioner, cracked the christening champagne bottle against the ferry at the launch ceremony on May 16, 1965, just eighteen months after the assassination.

Levingston was contracted to build three *Kennedy*-class ferries. At the time, some Americans still blamed Texas for the president's death. Hiring a Texas shipyard to build *Kennedy*-class ferryboats became an issue. Levingston enjoyed an excellent reputation for building ferryboats. However, the fact that it was owned by the Malloy brothers, Irish-Catholics, was also a benefit. As Bob Murphy, Ed Malloy's nephew, once said, the Irish-Catholic ownership may not have meant much in Texas, but in New York and Boston it meant a lot. And for the workers at Levingston, it was an opportunity to show their respect for the nation's fallen leader. Until the arrival of the *Kennedy*, the boats were painted red and black, but starting with the *Kennedy*, they have been painted orange and blue—the official New York City colors—along with the other boats that were operating when the *Kennedy* was put into service.

There are several other stories about the ferries' colors. One is that the three *Kennedy*-class ferries were the first Staten Island ferries to be painted municipal orange so that they could be seen in heavy fog and snow. Back in Texas, where they were painted at the Levingston shipyard, the story told was that it was in honor of the University of Texas, whose colors are orange and white. Another story was that it was in honor of Orange, the home of Levingston Shipbuilding.

The building of the *John F. Kennedy* Staten Island ferry was one of the most historic shipbuilding projects in the history of Texas. The three Kennedy-class ferries were designed by Kindland & Drake marine architects and engineers in New York. The ferries cost an estimated $4.5 million each. At the time, Levingston had extensive experience building diesel-electric-powered ferries. It had built two for the Brooklyn-to-Staten Island route, and seven for Lake Maracaibo, Venezuela.

When the Kennedy-class Staten Island ferries left Orange, the ferries were rated at sixteen knots. The propulsion system was essentially identical to the typical American Diesel locomotive. Four General Motors 1,600-horsepower diesel engines powered them. Levingston old-timers like to tell stories of when they drove the ferry vessels from Orange to New York City, they would stop along the way for fuel and jokingly ask people for directions to New York. One Levingston retiree related a story about watching the opening scenes in the movie *Working Girl* with his two grandchildren. When the scenes aboard the *John F. Kennedy* came on, he proudly told his grandchildren that their grandpa had helped build that ferry. It was, he said, one of the proudest moments of his life.

In the opening scene of Mike Nichols's classic film *Working Girl*, Melanie Griffith and Joan Cusack are on the *John F. Kennedy* ferry. The film, also featuring Harrison Ford, Alec Baldwin, and Sigourney Weaver, was a big hit in 1988. The opening scene on the ferry is accompanied by Carly Simon's singing "Let the River Run," for which she received the Academy Award for Best Original Song in 1989. The movie was a box office hit.

Paul A. Mattingly Jr.

The *JFK* was in operation during one of the country's darkest hours: September 11, 2001. A story written for San Francisco Bay Crossings— "Staten Island Ferry: Quiet Hero of 911"—describes the terrorizing events as seen from the famous ferry. *"The massive double-ender ferry John F. Kennedy carries 3,500 people, but guiding it into its slip at the tip of Manhattan was nothing new for Captain Eddie Squire. He'd been at the helm of a Staten Island ferry for more than twenty years. But today was September 11, and from his wheelhouse Captain Squire could see smoke pouring from the World Trade Center. First Mate Frank DeFazio joined Captain Squire, and the two men prepared for the routine return trip to Staten Island from their perch high above New York harbor. The last stragglers were disembarking into Manhattan, and Captain Squire was set to give the order to cast off line, when suddenly he and First Mate Dedario heard what they both later described as an "unnatural" noise coming from the water direction. Snapping his head that way, Captain Squire found himself face to face with the second 757, hideously angled, slashing directly toward him at nearly eye height. Poleaxed, he watched— and felt—as it thundered directly over the John F. Kennedy and into the World Trade Center, just nine blocks behind him. Emergency workers and supplies were already assembling in Staten Island, and orders were given to the John F. Kennedy to return at once and bring them to the disaster scene. She was on her way back to Manhattan within forty-five minutes, with hundreds of firefighters and other rescuers aboard frantically changing into their uniforms on the trip over. Abandoning their civilian clothes where they lay, they rushed from the ferryboat the moment it touched Manhattan, many to their deaths when the buildings collapsed soon after. It was the sad duty of the John F. Kennedy's crew to collect the personal effects of the fallen heroes. "We put hundreds of shoes into plastic bags," said Captain Squire, a crazed look in his eye. "Every bit of equipment we had, we sent ashore. Then we took back the wounded, the refugees. All we had left to help them was one box of gloves. One box of gloves!* Source: www.baycrossings.com. Author Eddie Joyce.

274 residents of Staten Island were killed on 9/11.

Penn Johnson, naval architect for Levingston at the time of the building of the *John F. Kennedy* Staten Island ferry, tells about one of the test runs in the Gulf of Mexico when he drove the ferry. He said it would do eighteen knots with no passengers and was designed to come to a full stop in two and one-half lengths. They were fully aware that the currents and tides at the Battery Park terminal can sometimes be strong, and the ferry demanded excellent handling characteristics for continuous safe landings. It was eerie to hear the scream of those 4 GM 567c's to put the ship into reverse because the current grabbed the boat, threatening to send it into the pilings.

Don Covington, former president of Levingston, told me he had a church pew manufacturer in Waco, Texas, manufacture the wooden seats for the *John F. Kennedy*. Covington said he used the company twin-engine Beechcraft plane on numerous trips to Waco to work out the details of the seats. I guess we can say the *John F. Kennedy* has church pews for seating. The Coast Guard banned wooden seats for the newer ferry vessels, alleging a fire hazard.

The legendary stories passed down by Levingston employees are of the "glory days" of the ferries and tugs built for

New York harbor. What you hear is the talk of pride, having worked on such high-profile projects. Not only is the venerable *John F. Kennedy* Staten Island ferry a unique piece of history for people on Staten Island, but also for America. It is a marine icon noted for its elegant simplicity of design with a diesel-electric propulsion system. It has been called the prettiest, smoothest riding, and most dependable of all the Staten Island ferries. As it just surpasses over fifty years of continuous service, "Granddaddy," as some affectionately call it, is a symbol of historical work by working people who say, "they were just doing their job." Maybe, on full retirement, the boat might be turned into a floating museum?

12

What Happened with Iran

Before World War II, Levingston had built only four warships for fighting. In 1962, Mohammad Reza Shah Pahlavi, the Shah of Iran, asked the U.S. government for assistance under the Mutual Defense Assistance Program, which was created during the Cold War to help those fighting communism and the Russians. The United States would pay for the military equipment that was bought from U.S. manufacturers through our military branches. President John F. Kennedy had agreed in 1962 to provide four "corvette" frigates to the Shah, considered "our man" and "guardian of the Persian Gulf." The monarch was credited as such due to the British Intelligence and the CIA overthrow of a democratically elected prime minister, Mohammed Mossadegh.

Mossadegh had nationalized the Anglo-Persian Oil Company, now known as BP, but then owned by the British government and the only oil company in Iran. They had found oil in 1908, only a few years after Spindletop. It has been written that John Foster Dulles and his brother Allen Dulles supported this overthrow over concern about Iran becoming a communist country. The CIA-orchestrated overthrow of Iran's prime minister in 1953 was allegedly organized by CIA officer, Kermit "Kim" Roosevelt, grandson of President Theodore Roosevelt.

With the commitment from President Kennedy to pay for the four ships to be built in America, the Iranians had done extensive research and settled on an Italian ship architect. I suspect that since the American taxpayer would foot the bill, they wanted nothing but the best. When the U.S. Navy suggested that one of their shipyard contractors build the ship, the Iranians balked.

They had determined that Levingston had the best capability to build their state-of-the-art ships. The warships were corvettes—small, fast patrol vessels that are typically lightly armed and used for shoreline patrolling. The design called for extensive use of aluminum to cut weight and to increase the performance of the ships. Levingston was known to have the best welders, including the ability to weld aluminum to steel. They were completed and delivered to Iran in 1964–1966. It is significant to note that in January of 1968 Britain announced its decision to withdraw from the Persian Gulf by 1971. This ended British protectorate and military presence in the Persian Gulf. The Persian Gulf Residency was an official colonial subdivision of the British Empire from 1763 until 1971, whereby the United Kingdom maintained varying degrees of political and economic control over several states in the Persian Gulf, including what is today known as the United Arab Emirates (formerly called the "Trucial Coast

States") and at various times southern portions of Persia, as well as Bahrain, Kuwait, Oman, and Qatar.

The people at Levingston felt that the Shah had a real appetite for the most extreme advanced weapons. The four corvette warships Levingston built for Iran were a milestone in the beginning of the Iranian military build-up, for which the equipment and sponsorship came from the United States. From working with the Iranian officers during construction of the corvettes, Levingston people told me that there was no doubt in their minds that the Shah appeared to be planning to militarily dominate the Persian Gulf with a modern navy and air force. The intent was to replace the British Empire's navy in the Persian Gulf. The Shah was encouraged and supported with U.S. equipment and personnel. The Levingston warships were a major step in the beginning of this process. In fact, in 1964, as part of the military cooperation with Washington, Iran's parliament passed a bill that made American military personnel and their families living in Iran immune from criminal prosecution. This created an issue with critics such as Ayatollah Ruhollah Khomeini in political circles.

Levingston never got another warship contract from the U.S. Navy. Since then the United States has invested billions and billions in naval warships, naval bases, and operational expenses to control the Persian Gulf. Iran suffered devastating losses from the Iraq invasion (1982) backed by the United States. The war cost both sides in lives and economic damage: half a million Iraqi and Iranian soldiers, with an equivalent number of civilians, are believed to have died, with many more injured; however, the war brought neither reparations nor changes in borders.

Fifty years from the time the four Levingston corvettes were sent to Iran, we see increasingly more killings and maiming in the countries adjoining the Persian Gulf. We know what has and is happening in Iraq, but the Iranian people have suffered intense oppression from the ruling Islamic government. Executions by the Iranian government against its own people have been a horrific tale of unbelievable cruelty. Yet most Americans know little about the Iranian people except what we are fed by special interests who are promoting war spending.

The United States was assuming the role as "guardian of the Gulf" and the role was made easy after the withdrawal of British forces east of the Suez in 1968. Initially, U.S. Naval forces in the region were negligible as the government chose to rely on the "Twin Pillars" of Iran and Saudi Arabia to provide security for the Gulf. This rationale quickly changed with the fall of the Shah of Iran (1979) and the Islamic Revolution with Ayatollah Ruhollah Khomeini as its leader, and for a decade Iran convulsed with violence and privation. It is speculated that the revolution was primarily caused by dissatisfaction with the autocratic rule of the Shah and his excessive spending on military armament. One story was that the honking of horns bothered the Shah, so he had the horn wiring cut on all autos.

The strong ties between Israel and Iran were also cut by the Iranian revolution in 1979. Iran closed the Israeli trade mission in Tehran, which had operated as a de facto embassy, and Ayatollah Ruhollah Khomeini dubbed Israel "an enemy of Islam." One story is that Iran blamed Israel for its partnership with the United States in support of the Shah.

Ayatollah Khomeini, on April 1, 1979, declared it the "first day of God's government." He obtained the title of "Imam," the highest religious rank in Shia Islam. With the establishment of the Islamic Republic of Iran, he became Supreme Leader (Vali-e Faqih).

Shortly thereafter, the Iraq-Iran bloodbath of a war started and lasted nearly eight years, from September of 1980 until August of 1988. It ended when Iran accepted United Nations (UN) Security Council Resolution 598, leading to an August 28, 1988, cease-fire. Iraq used chemical weapons with deadly force in 1988. Casualty figures are highly uncertain. The common belief is that there were more than one and a half million war and war-related casualties. The Iraqis suffered an estimated 375,000 casualties. Another 60,000 were taken prisoner by the Iranians. The war claimed at least 300,000 Iranian lives and injured more than 500,000. Nothing was settled, only a truce.

At the time of the Levingston-built naval patrol vessels, the relations between the United States and Israel with Iran were very close. Later, two of the Levingston-built patrol vessels were sunk by the U.S. Airforce in the Iraq-Iran war. The other two are still operating in the Iranian Navy.

From the time of the Iranian Revolution in 1979, the U.S. military has been actively involved in combat in the region starting with the Iran-Iraq War until today. The question is what will the future be? Historian and Arabism Professor

Jean-Pierre Filiu argues that terrorist groups like ISIS grew from the strategies and brutal tactics employed by Middle Eastern autocrats determined to hold onto power at any cost.

13

Pioneering Marine Offshore Rigs

From the 1950's to the 1970's, America's increasing demand for petroleum pushed the oil and gas industry further offshore in search of new reserves. It was an exciting and amazing time, considering that everyone was starting with a blank sheet of paper. It took a kind of innovation requiring a willingness to take risks. The thinking was bold and eager to apply creative approaches to hard problems. Offshore oil drilling has proven to be a true feast or famine business. When trying to survive the rough waters in a storm, it doesn't help to know that at some time the waters will be flat.

Levingston claimed the distinction as the only U.S. shipyard to build all five types of offshore drilling rigs: drill barges, submersibles, jack-ups, semisubmersibles, and drillships. Levingston became known as "the oilfield shipyard" and built 171 different offshore marine vessels in the three decades after the war.

Levingston built a tank basin for testing offshore models, aiming at a reliable prediction for meeting challenging wind and waves. In the pioneering days, Levingston was directly involved in exploring marine offshore equipment possibilities with concept development. Many of the basic concepts developed in those pioneering days are still used. In the immediate postwar years, Levingston invested heavily in equipment, engineering, research, and craftsmen. This required a continuous backlog of work and innovation to drive new designs to meet the demands of the growing offshore oil industry. It also meant the hiring and training of a new group of skilled workers. Cajun migrants from south Louisiana helped to fill the gap.

As the offshore industry evolved, exploration and production companies had to deal with significant environmental challenges: wind, currents, waves, and hurricanes. Over time, the industry learned painful lessons about hurricanes and applied new knowledge about weather and underwater soil conditions to build more efficient and safer systems. The basic question was what kind of marine and drilling platform was the best solution. Hurricanes slamming into the Gulf Coast in the 1960's shocked the industry with significant damages. Hurricane Camille in 1969 produced waves more than seventy feet high. Hurricane Katrina produced waves around one hundred feet off the coast of Mississippi. These storms were a strong wakeup call and forced companies and designers to address not only wave height, but also the time between the wave peaks. The original rig designers had no examples or experiences to go by, so novelty and innovation were the course of the day.

It was an exciting and risky time. The shipyards became early centers for experimenting with and advancing marine and offshore engineering. Industry had adapted technology first used in the wetlands for offshore operations. Most of the submersible drilling rigs of the early 1960's had the capacity to drill at depths no greater than eighty feet. As the industry moved further offshore into deeper waters, it required new technologies.

With its experience at building barges and tugs for major oil companies such as Humble Oil and Shell in the 1930's, and its core group of skilled engineers and yard supervisors, Levingston had a running start in the new construction market for offshore vessels in years following World War II. By the close of the 1940's, Levingston had built half a dozen drill barges. The largest was the drilling barge *Keystone*, Richardson & Bass rig No. 25, one of the largest barge-mounted steam rigs. It was designed and assembled specifically for drilling below 20,000 ft. The barge set consists of two separate barges connected as a unit by a catwalk, the drilling barge measuring 140 ft. by 54 ft. by 12 ft. and the boiler barge measuring 100 ft. by 27 ft. by 12 ft. The barges were built in 1946 by Levingston. Rigging-up commenced in October 1946, and the completed rig left the shipyard in January 1947.

In the late 1940's, a few oil companies, such as Humble Oil, Shell, Union Oil, The California Company, Superior Oil, and Pure Oil, were willing to tackle the offshore world. In 1947, Union Oil decided to get out of the drilling business. They sold the drilling operation to the employees for $750,000. To buy the assets, they had formed Santa Fe Drilling Company. The company enjoyed phenomenal success, expanding from the California oilfields to all over the world, changing their name to Santa Fe International. Expanding into offshore drilling, oil and gas exploration, and marine construction, they were bought by Kuwait Petroleum Company (KPC). The company was sold for cash in 1981. One dollar invested in 1947 by an employee for a share paid off to the tune of $2,244 in 1981.

Paul A. Mattingly Jr.

In 1954, a historical event took place in the offshore drilling business. Zapata Off-Shore Company was formed as a subsidiary of Zapata Oil. What makes this event historical is the fact that a thirty-year-old George Herbert Walker Bush was the president of the new company. He raised some startup money from Eugene Meyer, publisher of the *Washington Post*, and Meyer's son-in-law, Phillip Graham. Zapata Off-Shore accepted an offer from an inventor, R. G. LeTourneau, for the development of a mobile, but secure, drilling rig. Zapata advanced him $400,000, which was to be refundable if the completed rig did not function.

Robert Fogal, Sr., George H.W. Bush, and Mrs. Robert Fogal at the Levingston Shipyard for a launching. Courtesy of the Fogal Family. 1965

Bush had Levingston do numerous repair and new build jobs until 1966, when he sold his interest to a group including his business partner, Robert Gow. Afterwards, he had an unsuccessful bid for Congress.

The sellers of Zapata Off-Shore took a note for $3.2 million. One of the new investors was William S. Farrish III, an heir to the Humble Oil & Refining Co./Standard Oil of New Jersey fortune. Four years later the assets were built up to an estimated value of $361 million. Zapata sold its offshore marine equipment in 1990, and it was resold to Diamond Offshore Drilling, Inc. in 1995.

Global Marine Drilling Company started in 1958 with employees of Union Oil. In the sixties, it produced the first operational drillships that have proven to be a gigantic leap in marine drilling. Levingston built eight of the drillships in the 1960's and 1970's.

Global filed Chapter 11 Bankruptcy in 1986 when the price of oil collapsed. A few years later, Global Marine emerged from bankruptcy, and in 2001, they became a wholly owned unit of Santa Fe, while Santa Fe was renamed on July 23, 2007. A merger between Global Santa Fe and larger rival Transocean was announced. The merger was completed on November 27, 2007. The combined company is also known as Transocean.

The major oil companies shifted to independent drilling contractors in the 1950's. These companies dealt with new, untested designs and had to constantly change their technology and innovate. "The oil companies did not have the expertise to build anything...but they had a problem and they needed us to solve it," stated Larry Baker Sr., former manager at Levingston and founder of Baker Marine Company. "And they had the money to solve that problem. And Levingston developed the people to carry with this further and further and further out into deeper water."

In 1947, Kerr-McGee Oil Industries drilled the first productive well "out-of-sight-of-land," on a platform located 10.5 miles off the Louisiana coast in the Ship Shoal area. This platform, called the *Kermac 16*, was supported by a drilling tender (named after the coal-carrying tenders coupled to steam train engines), the *Frank Phillips*, a Navy surplus YF barge converted by Levingston Shipbuilding Company. At the dawn of the offshore business, Levingston converted several of these former military ships to drilling tenders.

Senator Bob Kerr, Hugh McGee, Kerr's brother, T. W. Fentern. Kerr McGee Oil Industries. 1947.

By the early 1950's, after years of difficult weather, the new marine environment, and years of political bickering between the states and the federal government over territorial rights to offshore waters, the offshore oil and gas development program, known as the Outer Continental Shelf (OCS), took off at a rapid pace. Observers labeled this offshore program "the biggest gamble of them all."

W. M. Keck, Sr. Courtesy of Beaumont Photo

In 1952 Levingston delivered the *W. M. Keck, Sr.*, a state-of-the-art drill barge built for Superior Oil Company to drill offshore in the Gulf of Mexico. This is the same W. M. Keck who founded the Superior Oil Company and the W.M. Keck Foundation in 1954 in Los Angeles. It is one of the nation's largest philanthropic organizations, with assets of more than $1.2 billion. The W. M. Keck Foundation supports outstanding science, engineering, and medical research and undergraduate education. The scale model of the 1952 drilling barge, *W. M. Keck, Sr.*, is in the boardroom of the offices.

Among the platform tenders built by Levingston was the $1.5 million, *F.A. Cleverly*, delivered in 1955. By the end of the decade, Levingston had constructed more than twenty marine vessels for service offshore. Such projects quickly led to others. Levingston constructed its first self-contained drill barge in August 1955 and its first pipe laying barge in June 1958.

Soon, Levingston's leaders saw the need to expand its facilities to meet the needs of its customers. The firm had a long-term lease on an eighty-acre island across the Sabine River in Louisiana owned by the B.E. Quinn family of Beaumont, Texas. This island, called Harbor Island, ultimately served as a major fabrication center for many of Levingston's offshore drilling rigs and marine vessels. However, all employees, equipment, electricity, and other utilities had to cross the Sabine River to reach the island facility every day. This move also required a separate accounting to record activity and taxes for the State of Louisiana separate from the existing six acres on the mainland in the State of Texas. Levingston became a Louisiana based company. This decision to expand to the island was a wholehearted commitment by Levingston to go all out as a pioneer in the offshore rig building business. The oil industry has a tradition of being extremely conservative in the innovation of business practices and in adoption of new technology. There is an inherent fear of change.

One of the exceptions was C. H. Murphy, Jr., president of Murphy Oil, who bankrolled the first jack-up, *Mr. Charlie*, named after him. Alden "Doc" Laborde, a former superintendent for an offshore oil company, came up with the idea for a submersible drilling barge that would take offshore rigs out into deep waters. Charles H. Murphy, Jr., along with some investors from St. Louis, backed Laborde's project. The prototype, *Mr. Charlie*, commenced drilling operations in June 1954 for Shell Oil Co. and helped revolutionize the offshore business.

Laborde was recognized as one of the pioneers in the offshore oil industry. He was from a prominent Catholic French family. A native of Vinton, Louisiana, who grew up in Marksville, Louisiana, Laborde graduated from the U.S. Naval Academy in 1938. Laborde, who had served in the Navy during World War II, started in the offshore industry in 1946 as a marine superintendent representing the owners of one of the first major drill barges, *Keystone*, for the Richardson/Bass group out of Fort Worth, while the rig was under construction at the Levingston shipyard. The drill barge was nicknamed the "swamp barge" because it was designed to drill in the coastal marshes and swamplands of south Louisiana. The *Keystone* drill barge was a major step in having a drilling rig on a movable barge. Laborde took his experience from overseeing the construction at Levingston and went to work for Kerr-McGee, one of the first companies to venture into the offshore waters of the Gulf. When Laborde and his brother, John, founded Tidewater Marine, they asked my dad, Paul A. Mattingly, Jr., to join them. But my mother did not want to move from Houston to New Orleans.

Laborde ended up starting three companies, including an oil drilling company named Ocean Drilling and Exploration Co. (ODECO). In 1994, it became part of Diamond Offshore

Drilling, Inc. The primary investor for ODECO was an Arkansas oilman named Charley Murphy. Murphy invested $500,000 toward a new type of drilling rig named after him and helped get other investors. The innovative new type of rig allowed ODECO to become a leader in offshore drilling. The other company Laborde founded was Tidewater Marine Service Corporation with John Laborde, his brother, as president. Today, with a fleet of more than 350 vessels, Tidewater is one of the oldest and most experienced names in the offshore marine industry.

Levingston's most valuable customer was Brown & Root. These pioneers of offshore construction had the utmost confidence in Levingston to produce high-quality offshore vessels and renovate them. This is reflected in the construction of a 150-foot vessel named *Margarett Root II*, named for the wife of Herman Brown, who founded Brown & Root. Herman Brown, remembered as a "working man's man," personally visited the job site throughout the year and often spent time with his employees rather than his executives. The other half of the company's name came from Brown's brother-in-law, Dan Root, Margarett's brother. Root died a few years after the founding of the company in 1919, but his name continued.

The *Margarett Root II* was classified as a 289-ton survey/research vessel. The vessel was a deep-sea fishing boat for executives of Brown & Root. It was outfitted with the most luxurious accommodations and accessorized with teakwood trim and brass fittings. Levingston was sworn to secrecy about the cost and purpose of the vessel. Levingston's cost accounting records were comingled with another Brown & Root job to hide the true cost. George Bolin, Houston real estate broker, who is known for large iconic real estate deals, told me that when his father, L. J. Bolin, longtime Brown & Root executive, took him along on a *Margarett Root II* snapper fishing trip, he was amazed at the luxurious finishing. The one thing he distinctly remembered was the central air conditioning system. The prior vessel, *Margarett Root I*, had no air conditioning. When he asked his father what the vessel cost, he was told over $3 million dollars. In 2016 dollars, that was $25 million. This was Levingston's only venture into building a luxury fishing yacht. The vessel's name was changed in 1993 to the *Delta Queen* and was flagged in the United Arab Emirates.

The Browns were very knowledgeable about shipbuilding. They established Brown Shipbuilding, a separate company from Brown & Root, Inc. in 1941 at the junction of Green's Bayou in Houston. Herman Brown selected young L. T. Bolin to buy the 146-acre tract and run the new shipbuilding company. Bolin was one of the top executives at Brown & Root until he retired. Bolin was the ultimate construction man, with a cigar always in his mouth.

My favorite story about Herman Brown is the one told to me by a retired Brown & Root employee. It concerned the greenhouse next to the corporate offices in Houston. The most beautiful flowers were grown there. Every morning, flowers would be picked and arranged in a bouquet. Then they would be taken to Herman Brown's home and placed on the breakfast table for his wife, Margarett.

The Brown's had two adopted children, Mike Stude and Louisa Stude Sarofim, who, with the heirs of George Brown, are community leaders helping to direct $50 million a year in charitable grants from the Brown Foundation established by George and Herman Brown. It is a $1 billion foundation that has granted over $1.2 billion from 1951 through 2011. The Margarett Root Brown College, established at Rice University, is often shortened to the name Brown College. Interestingly, the Brown Foundation was rated as the sixty-third largest foundation in America in 2014.

The sixty-second largest foundation is the Samuel Noble Foundation and the sixty-first is the W. M. Keck Foundation. Levingston built a jack-up rig for Noble Drilling named the *Sam Noble*. They also built the *W.M. Keck Sr.,* for Superior Oil. Levingston built several vessels named after the Brown Foundation's founders.

On February 23, 1950, Lloyd Noble, founder of Noble Drilling, died at the age of 53. In addition to the Samuel Noble Foundation named after his father, Lloyd's will named 106 other beneficiaries, including his housekeeper and some of his employees' children. Throughout his life, Noble taught a simple tenet, one that remains a guiding principle seven decades later. He believed all great accomplishments begin the same way – with a dedicated team that builds together. It was also said that Lloyd Noble believed that when the precious resource of oil is depleted, that humans will still need to eat. Founded in 1945, the Noble Foundation conducts direct operations, including assisting farmers and ranchers, and conducting plant science research and agricultural programs, to enhance agricultural productivity regionally, nationally, and internationally.

The stories of these foundations are examples of the legacies of some of the outstanding pioneers in the offshore oil business. These are just a few examples of their giving back to humankind.

14

Herbert Hunt

Another one of Levingston's best customers was the Penrod Drilling Company. Penrod was founded in late 1936 by H. L. Hunt as a contract drilling company. He had given the ownership of the company in a trust to his children: Nelson Bunker Hunt, Lamar Hunt, Herbert Hunt, Caroline Hunt, H. L. "Hassie" Hunt III, and Margaret Hunt. Herbert, Lamar, and Nelson Bunker bought Penrod.

Herbert Hunt explained that when his dad started the small drilling company in the 1930's, he asked his young daughter, Caroline, if she wanted to name the company. She told him that she liked the name "Penrod" from a children's book about an eleven-year-old boy growing up. Hunt explained that they have used the combination of six letters starting with a "P" for numerous corporate names such as Placid Oil. Petro-Hunt was an LLC formed by Herbert Hunt, who has also used such names as Purity, Pillar, and Pursue in establishing companies for his family. An interesting side note is that Ramona Stark, the daughter of Edgar Brown, Jr.'s second cousin, Homer Stark, married Caroline's son, John Bunker Sands.

As Nelson's interest shifted to drilling for oil in the Middle East, while Lamar was forming the American Football League and founding the Kansas City Chiefs, it fell to Herbert to run Penrod. Lamar is credited with coming up with the name "Super Bowl" for the national championship game. In 1972, he became the first American Football League personage inducted into the Pro Football Hall of Fame.

Under Herbert's guidance, Penrod made the transition into offshore drilling. In the late 1940's, the company built a series of shallow-water inland drill barges to drill the shallow bays of Louisiana. In 1954, Levingston built the first drill barges for Penrod to drill offshore. Herbert Hunt once said that the reason Penrod chose Levingston was because of the shipyard's reputation as a pioneer in the marine business. Also, Levingston had a large dry dock that allowed the company to build drill barges in a cheaper and more efficient manner. The first such vessel for Penrod was named *Jim Garrison*, one of the first drillers for H. L. Hunt. Later, Levingston delivered the *Penrod 45*, which was christened by Caroline Hunt, wife of Nelson Bunker Hunt. The ceremony was also attended by Lamar and Herbert. Through the decades, the relationship between the people at Levingston and Penrod grew stronger. Some of Penrod's drilling rigs were built by Far East Levingston (Keppel FELS) in Singapore.

Under the leadership of Herbert Hunt, in the mid-1980's Penrod became one of the industry's largest offshore drilling contractors. Penrod was noted for loyalty to and from employees and superior in-house training and mentoring.

A Penrod employee, Clarence Hebert, wrote in a company newsletter to employees, "When times get tough, the tough get going. Well, times are tough, so let's get going, doing the best possible job for our employer by being the best at the specific job assigned and be prepared to assume additional responsibility when the time comes." In the oil bust of the 1980's, a traumatic halt was brought to offshore drilling. Penrod was taken over by Richard Rainwater who, in 1993, renamed the company Ensco. Today, Ensco is ranked as the second largest offshore drilling company in the world.

Herbert Hunt was a major customer of Levingston. Recently, I asked Hunt what kind of legal contracts they had with Levingston when they built the first drill barges. He replied they didn't have one. They used a letter of understanding for the deal. He laughed and commented, "Those days are gone." At eighty-six, Herbert Hunt has been at the top of the oil business for many decades.

In 1961, Herbert and his brothers discovered one of the largest oilfields in the world on their lease in Libya—the Sarir Field. George Williamson, my son-in-law's uncle, had negotiated the lease deal for the Hunts in a tent in 1957. It was an oil lease for the Hunt brothers for the Sarir field, which has produced to this day over six billion barrels of oil. The Hunt brothers had eight million acres of oilfields under lease in Libya. It took them about six years to produce oil from the field and required the building of new infrastructure: production equipment, storage, pipelines, and terminals to sell the oil. They brought in British Petroleum (BP) for a 50 percent interest as the operating partner for money and resources. After five years of production, Libya's ruler, Muammar Gaddafi nationalized the field in 1973.

As noted, the Sarir Field was discovered in 1961. It is bigger than the legendary East Texas Oil Field. Per Herbert Hunt, the oilfield has produced over 6.5 billion barrels of oil, more oil than the famous East Texas oilfields, which, ironically, were largely developed by his father, the late H. L. Hunt. Later, when he and his brothers invested in silver, the government changed the rules, causing a deliberate crash in silver prices, and the Hunt Brothers had to declare personal bankruptcy. From these ashes of failure, W. Herbert Hunt returned as a true oil wildcatter with amazing success in the new technologically advanced shale rock oil boom. Per *Forbes* magazine, Hunt is now a multi-billionaire. Hunt has created a network of two hundred companies filing federal tax returns for his family. As he sits in his new offices at Petro-Hunt LLC, one of the largest privately held companies in the world, and remains active in the onshore and offshore sectors of the energy industry, Hunt denies *Forbes*'s wealth estimates, saying, "I am only a consultant to the companies run by my children and grandchildren."

What a special invitation it was when Herbert Hunt asked me to join him for lunch. Of course, he has his own chefs for all the Petro-Hunt employees—in a company cafeteria in one big room. We sat at the table with his two sons and three grandchildren. They discussed business, told funny stories, and were very friendly. Employees would come up to the table and visit. It was like one big family. How very different from the fancy restaurants and private dining rooms of corporate America. In our discussions about the oil business, Herbert Hunt explained oil prices in this way: "I have seen oil sell for as little as ten cents a barrel and as high as $143 a barrel." The message I got from this was that you must always consider a wide range of possibilities. Bunker, Herbert, and Lamar, gambling boldly on rising inflation, bet their collective shares of their fortune on real estate, energy, agriculture, and commodities during the 1970's. At one point, their net worth was estimated as high as $14 billion. At today's value, that would equal $60 billion. Their debacle in the silver market cost them $1.5 billion in 1980 and devastated their fortunes. But the loss of oil rights in Libya hit their business the most. The Hunt legacy defines the wildcatter spirit. Some made billions, others lost everything. Besides being one of the early pioneers in offshore drilling, Herbert Hunt is considered one of the great Texas wildcatters.

While discussing Cajuns with Herbert Hunt, I mentioned how they live in south Louisiana and work all over the world in the oil industry. Hunt laughed and told me about sending workers overseas to work for Penrod. The work schedule was seven days on and seven days off. This was the only way the workers would agree to go overseas and still maintain their residences back in Louisiana. Hunt said that when he traveled abroad, he was constantly running into Penrod employees on planes. There came a time when costs needed to be cut and the schedules were changed to fourteen days on and fourteen days off. They were pleasantly surprised that the workers preferred this, saying it gave them more time with their families and less time traveling. Today, a typical schedule on offshore rigs is a rotational schedule of twenty-one days on, twenty-one days off, when working in most positions in the U.S. Gulf of Mexico. Longer rotations are more typical for international work.

15

The "Cadillac" of Rigs

Mary Jane Noble had the honor of christening the rig named after her husband and father-in-law. The self-elevating, offshore drilling unit *Sam Noble*, built by Levingston Shipbuilding Company of Orange, Texas, was christened in January 1983 in ceremonies held in Port Arthur, Texas. The unit was built for the Noble Drilling Corporation, and was christened by Mrs. Mary Jane Noble, wife of Sam Noble, chairman of the board of Noble Affiliates, Inc. The *Sam Noble* is a Levingston Class 111-C rig capable of drilling to 25,000 feet in water depths of up to 300 feet. The sister ship of the *Ed Holt*, which was christened by Levingston a year before, the *Sam Noble* was designed with capabilities for duty in international and remote locations.

In 2015, the company was ranked number 505 on the Fortune 1000. Noble Energy, Inc., formerly Noble Affiliates, Inc., is a petroleum exploration and production company headquartered in Houston, Texas. In 1932, Lloyd Noble founded the Samedan Oil Corporation, predecessor company to Noble Energy, Inc. The company was named after his children Sam, Ed, and Ann.

At the christening of the *Sam Noble,* Levingston president, Don Covington, gave a speech on behalf of the Levingston group, which surprisingly turned out to be a farewell speech to the company. Anybody who ever attended a christening at Levingston remembers it as an unforgettable experience, and this one was even more memorable. The atmosphere and passion of the people involved created a spirit of celebration that few would ever forget. Levingston was famous for christenings, with great food—usually boiled shrimp and raw oysters. The rig was finished at Gulfport Shipbuilding in Port Arthur, Texas. Gulfport was purchased in the early 1970's by Levingston from Bruno Schultz. Schultz was an immigrant from Germany who founded Gulfport Shipyard in the 1930's.

Spin-offs of this pioneering design were the Baker Marine-designed jack-ups. Baker Marine was founded by ex-Levingston employees in 1975. Baker Marine designed an impressive sixty-two jackup rigs. Keppel FELS took the Levingston designs and improved them with patented proprietary advancements. Keppel FELS has built the most jack-up rigs of any shipbuilding company in the world.

Keppel FELS used their own proprietary concepts to design and build the *Seafox 5* (2013), a four-legged, self-elevating, self-propelled jack-up unit for accommodation, construction, transportation, installation, maintenance, and good services with a giant crane able to lift 1,200 tons and work in water depths of 300 feet (91 meters). The unit offers permanent accommodation for 150 people.

Seafox 5 is operated by the Seafox Group, a Netherlands-based firm that operates in the offshore energy field, doing jobs such as installing offshore wind foundations. This is just one example of the many successful Keppel FELS proprietary concepts for customers. As the demand for offshore drilling rigs periodically goes into a massive downward slump, an offshore rig builder needs alternative markets to survive. Keppel FELS conducts offshore wind energy research on self-installing platforms for substations, turbine foundations, wind turbine installation vessels and cable laying vessels.

Per the Bureau of Ocean Energy Management (BOEM) Washington D.C., many countries, including the United States, have coastal areas with high wind resource potential. Worldwide there are 4.45 GW of offshore wind energy installed, with another 4.72 GW under construction and an additional 30.44 GW approved. GW stands for a gigawatt of power which will provide enough energy for 700,000 homes. An assumption is that a typical home uses about 11,000 kilowatts per year.

Photo Titles in Sequence
(1) If You Work Here…
(2) *Sea Otter II*…
(3) Offshore Barge…
(4) One of Moran's "Cadillacs"
(5) Hydrogen Explosion…
(6) Wives at Levingston…
(7) H.L. Hunt's Sons…

(8) Levingston Leaders
(9) Iranian Navy
(10) "Happy Trails…"
(11) George H.W. Bush…
(12) Don Covington…
(13) Margarett Root
(14) The Iconic *John F. Kennedy*…
(15) Frozen Heat
(16) The New York Wheel
(17) Chikyu…
(18) Diamonds Are Forever
(19) Shangri-La

If You Work Here, You Know You're Good!

July 15, 1942. Photo: Gunn Photo-*Orange Leader*

The photo says it all. Leadership, talented work force, team spirit and pride in one's work. Edgar W. Brown, Jr. provided the leadership and capital to build a wartime shipyard. Levingston was a unique shipyard that designed their own ocean rescue tugs and sold them to the U.S. Navy. Given a special classification of Auxiliary Tugs or ATA, ninety were built in Orange and 22 were built by Gulfport Shipbuilding Co. in Port Arthur, Texas.

The ocean rescue tugs were attached to U.S., British and Russian convoys, and partook in other projects such as the Normandy Invasion. One of the tugboats, renamed *R/V Horizon*, was the first boat to take the Scripps Institution of Oceanography to blue waters.

Sea Otter II, Experimental Cargo Ship

Business Men's Studio, of Beaumont, Texas. Photograph #10769, 1941. Sea Otter II built as a prototype for the Army during WWII by Levingston Shipbuilding Company of Orange, Texas. Photograph from the Ed T. and Marjorie H. Malloy Archives at the Sam Houston Regional Library and Research Center, P.O. Box 310, Liberty, Texas 77575. Telephone, 936-336-8821.

The IX-53 specification contract was granted June 24, 1941, to Levingston Shipbuilding, in Orange, Texas. The experimental freighter named *Sea Otter II* was delivered on October 26, 1941. It was built on a guarantee to complete in a few months requiring a 24-hours-a-day, seven-days-a-week schedule. The experimental project was hatched in the Oval Office by President Franklin D. Roosevelt. It was fought by the U.S. Navy which did not want to build experimental merchant marine ships. The vessel had many design flaws and became known as a "folly," and President Roosevelt suffered wide criticism in the news media for the failed project. The vessel had four screws with a total of sixteen Chrysler gasoline engines. The design was incomplete and needed extensive changes.

It is historical to be able to document the fact that a President was behind an experimental project. Roosevelt came up with a lend-lease program for England to buy the *Sea Otter II* freighter.

Offshore Barge Drills Below 20,000 Feet

Otho Haunschild, left, and Paul Mattingly, Sr., discuss the *Keystone* drill barge no. 25, built for Sid Richardson and the Bass Brothers. It was designed to drill to 20,000 feet. Richardson and Bass hired a WWII Navy officer, Lieutenant Commander Alden "Doc" Laborde, to oversee the job. Consisting of a drilling barge and a boiler barge, the completed rig was delivered by Levingston in January 1947, establishing the company as the leader in marine offshore drilling equipment.

Laborde later founded Odeco Drilling Company (renamed Diamond Drilling) with Murphy Oil Corp. founder, Charles Murphy, Jr. Later he founded Tidewater Marine and Gulf Island Fabrication, Inc.

Paul A. Mattingly Jr.

One of Moran's "Cadillacs"

Courtesy: Noble Maritime Collection. Noble lithograph

Built in 1949 by Levingston Shipbuilding Co., hull #442 was christened the *Doris Moran* for the famous Moran Towing Company of New York, New York. Her "sister" diesel electric tugs built by Levingston were the *Grace Moran*, *Barbara Moran*, *Carol Moran*, and *Moira Moran*. They were referred to as "Moran's Cadillacs," after the very prestigious General Motor's automobile of that era.

Moran was founded in 1860. World War II initiated a period of rapid growth and geographic expansion for the company. When the United States returned to peacetime, Moran made some key decisions that enhanced its market position, providing a platform for future growth. The five diesel-electrics built by Levingston were a show of confidence in the economic future of America.

Hydrogen Explosion Wipes Out an Island

It was on the eve of Halloween, 1952, in the United States when American scientists set off a hydrogen explosion in the Marshall Islands. The "Ivy Mike" test had about 700 times the explosive power of the atomic bomb dropped on Hiroshima, Japan, seven years earlier, killing 160,000 people.

The ocean rescue tug USS ATA-180, built by Levingston for the Navy, was given to the Scripps Institution of Oceanography in 1948. It was renamed *R/V Horizon* and was the first vessel to be used for blue water ocean research. Located 72 nautical miles from the detonation site, it was the only civilian ship doing research for the explosion. They were monitoring wave action and tsunami development. The *Horizon* suffered low level radiation fallout.

Paul A. Mattingly Jr.

Wives at Levingston Christening

The tradition of christening a ship goes back centuries and is believed to bring good luck to the vessel. At the ceremony, the sponsor, a woman, is given the honor of breaking the traditional bottle of champagne against the bow just before the ship enters the water for the first time. Wives of some of the Levingston associates would dress up in their finest and join in the celebration. Adriana Ingram, in all white, sixth from the right, was the older sister of the famous football coach, Bum Philips. She is credited with giving him his nickname. On Adrian's left, fifth from the right, is Colette Malloy, the aunt of Sam Skinner, who was chief-of-staff for President George H.W. Bush. Skinner is the father-in-law of Roger Goodell, Commissioner for the National Football League (NFL).

H. L. Hunt's Sons at Levingston Christening

Photo: Businessman's Men's Studio Beaumont

The Bilge Club at the Levingston Shipyard. Left to right: Herbert, Lamar, and Nelson Bunker Hunt. At the far right is Walter Pennington and in the background is Richard Allen, both of Levingston.

The occasion was the christening by Jane Hunt of the drilling barge *John Garrison*, named for the original driller of Penrod Drilling Company. Penrod was led by Herbert Hunt, who grew it to become the largest drill contractor in the world. Today, it is part of Ensco, plc. His brother, Lamar was co-founder of the American Football league, merged to form the National Football League (NFL). He founded the Kansas City Chiefs and is credited with naming the championship NFL game "The Super Bowl." Nelson, led the oil drilling and production business for the Hunt Brothers.

Levingston Leaders

Business Men's Studio, of Beaumont, Texas, Photograph #29567-26. Photograph of the 1953 christening celebration of the Ferry Boat Carabobo, built for Compania de Transportes of Maracaibo, Venezuela. The boat was built by the Levingston Shipbuilding Company of Orange, Texas and sponsored by Mrs. Hortensia Shortt. Photograph from the Ed T. and Marjorie H. Malloy

The year was 1952. The location was in the Bilge Club, the private club at the Levingston Shipyard. Orange was a dry county, but the club was wet.

Left to right: Otho Haunschild, yard superintendent and later president of Levingston; Johnny Shortt, president of La Translacustre Co., Lake Maracaibo, Venezuela, and joint venture partner of the Maracaibo shipyard; Levingston officers Edward T. Malloy, President; Walter Pennington, Vice-President, and later President; Peter Bednar, Vice President-Engineering; Paul Mattingly, Sr., Chief Financial Officer; and at the far right, Clarence Levingston. It was a youthful group and proved the saying, "Youth and skill will win out every time over age and treachery."

Iranian Navy

President Kennedy committed to four "Corvettes" for the Shah of Iran, Mohammed Reza Shah Pahlavi. They were paid for by the military assistance program (MAP). The ships were built by Levingston Shipbuilding Co. in Orange and transferred by the U.S. Navy to Iran. The last one was completed on December 10, 1968. Note the missile launchers on the ship.

The "Corvettes" were state of the art with all the bells and whistles, including extra thick steel hulls and an aluminum interior structure for weight reduction. Levingston was a leader in aluminum/steel welding. The ships had the latest electronics and high performance diesel-electric propulsion.

Two of the ships were sunk in the Iran-Iraq war by the U.S. Air Force. The other two ships are still operating in the Iranian Navy. They are the only fighting warships that Levingston ever built.

"Happy Trails To You"

Photo courtesy of the Brown family and Houston Rodeo

Dale Evans was married to Roy Rogers, the "King of the Cowboys." They appeared together on television for decades and were well known for their theme song, "Happy Trails to You." Often, they were the star attraction at the Houston Livestock Show and Rodeo.

The man Evans is dancing with is not Roy Rogers. He is Edgar Brown, Jr. with a $100 bill as a bow-tie. When he controlled and led Levingston, he brought fun and excitement, particularly to the shipyard parties celebrating the launching of vessels. In Houston, he was a guiding force in the Houston Livestock Show and Rodeo. In 2016, the charitable organization contributed over $24.8 million in donations to scholarships for youths and youth programs. Since 1932, the organization's total contributions have been $420 million.

In 1974, the entire Houston Rodeo show was dedicated to Edgar Brown.

George H. W. Bush at Levingston

At the wave pool testing scale models used in creating designs.

At the far left is George H. W. Bush with his arms folded. The watch on his wrist is the one he was wearing when his plane was shot down in World War II. He was the only survivor of his 3-man crew. To his left are three Zapata associates. On the far right is Robert Fogal, Jr., Don Covington, and Robert Fogal, Sr., all of Levingston.

The study of wave sizes is very important in the offshore drilling industry. How high do waves go? In 2005, the estimated highest wave height during Hurricane Katrina was 106 feet, south of Dauphine, Alabama.

Don Covington, Great Pioneer of Offshore Oil

Photo: Paul A. Mattingly Jr. Collection

Don Covington has 70 years of working experience in the marine offshore industry. His father-in-law was an executive at Levingston, and his father had worked there, as well. Don's brother-in-law, Bob Fogal, Jr., also worked at Levingston, as did his son, Robert Fogal III, who is now an engineering manager with Transocean. Levingston has been truly a family affair in the Covington family.

The photo on the wall is the Levingston Class-111C jackup rig named *Sam Noble* in honor of the President of Noble Drilling Co. The name is also on the Sam Noble Museum of Natural History in Norman, Oklahoma, one of the finest natural history museums in the world. The Sam Noble Foundation, with over a billion dollars in assets, is focused on agricultural research and practices.

Margarett Root

Photo: George Bolin collection

The *Margarett Root II*, about 150 feet long, was "called" an offshore supply boat and was built by Levingston Shipbuilding Company in 1969. It was not an offshore supply boat. It was a luxury ocean fishing boat designed for entertaining on offshore fishing trips. The cost of the vessel was "secret."

The name, *Margarett Root II*, was in honor of Herman Brown's wife. Brown had co-founded Brown & Root in 1919 with his wife's brother, Daniel Root, who supplied the money. Root soon died, but his name stayed on in the company.

Margarett Root Brown is best known in Texas for the Brown Foundation she founded with her husband and his brother, George Brown, and wife Alice. Through 2014, the Brown Foundation has given $1.5 billion in grants.

Paul A. Mattingly Jr.

The Iconic *John F. Kennedy* Staten Island Ferry

Photo: Paul Mattingly collection

A NYC tourist highlight from Manhattan to Staten Island is the short 5.2-mile ferry ride which offers a fantastic view of the Manhattan skyline and the Statue of Liberty.

A piece of Levingston Shipbuilding Company is part of the NYC scene. The Levingston-built *John F. Kennedy* ferry boat has been carrying passengers for over 50 years – since 1965.

The Staten Island Ferry Boat Company was founded by Staten Island resident, "Commodore" Cornelius Vanderbilt. It was his first business venture and led to his becoming the richest man in America.

The *John F. Kennedy* ferry boat has been an iconic star and was featured in the movie, *Working Girl*, directed by Mike Nichols and starring Harrison Ford, Sigourney Weaver, Melanie Griffith, and Alec Baldwin.

Frozen Heat

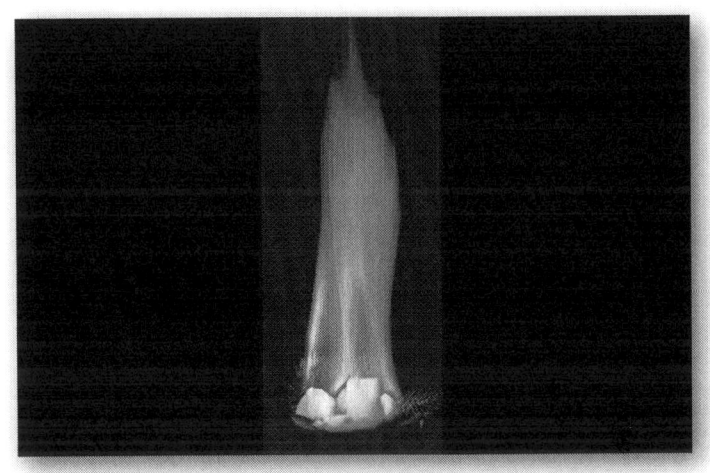

Photo: United States Geological Survey (USGS)

Frozen heat is ice that will burn like a candle when lighted with a match. Ice core was retrieved from beneath the Gulf of Mexico by the *Glomar Challenger* in the late 1970's. Packaged core samples were sent to the Colorado School of Mines for analysis. It was the first time for samples of gas (primarily methane) inside of ice to go to a scientific laboratory.

These ices are called gas hydrates, created by the reaction of gases—such as methane, ethane, and hydrogen sulfide—with water at low temperatures and high pressure to form a solid. A nickname for gas hydrates is "frozen heat." Today, it is looked upon as a potential for energy resources greater than all of the fossil fuels found on the planet. On the other hand, it has the potential to be released into the atmosphere because of warming from the permafrost, with devastating impact on life dependent on oxygen.

The New York Wheel

Credit: NY Wheel

An estimated 2 million tourists take the free ride on the Staten Island Ferry yearly to see New York Harbor from the water, an impressive view of the New York skyline, and a glimpse of the Statue of Liberty. On arrival at the ferry terminal in Staten Island, there is little to do and most tourists never leave the terminal.

That will change when the New York Observation Wheel opens sometime in 2017. At 630 feet in height, it is 89 feet taller than the Singapore Flyer (2008) and 80 feet taller than the new High Roller in Las Vegas. It will be the focal point of a newly developing "Centre" that will include restaurants, hotels, and apartments.

In 2012, Mayor Bloomberg has been quoted as saying that the development "will soon feature an attraction unlike any other in New York City -- in fact, it will be unlike any other on the planet."

From Orange To Singapore

Chikyu – the Japanese Word for Earth Discovery

Smithsonian Ocean Portal Sant Ocean Hall,
Washington, D.C. Scale model: Chikyu.

Owned by JAMESTEC - Japan Agency for Marine Earth Science and Technology - the *Chikyu* is a Japanese scientific drilling ship built for the IODP - Integrated Ocean Drilling Program. The *Chikyu* is being contributed to the IODP scientific community to better understand how the earth system operates and to help humankind make wise decisions for our future. The other ship in the IODP program is the *Joides Resolution* operated by Texas A&M University. These two ship are the legacy of the *Glomar Challenger*.

Diamonds Are Forever

Photo: courtesy of De Beers

The *Debmar Atlanta,* built by Levingston Shipbuilding and operating off the coast in South Africa. A large-scale model is displayed in the Houston Maritime Museum, Houston, Texas.

When you see a diamond, it might have been mined by a Levingston-built drillship. The world's richest marine diamond deposits were carried by the Orange River from the center of South Africa millions of years ago and deposited across the ocean floor. Namdeb Diamond Corp., which is owned by the Namibian government and Anglo American PlC De Beers, mined 1.76 million carats in 2013.

Shangri-La

Larry Baker, Sr., is still going strong at age 92 (2017). When he retired, he and his wife, Virginia, built a home in Lafayette Parish along the Vermillion Bayou. It is a replica of the eighteenth century historic "Linden" home in Natchez, Mississippi. The Bakers called the estate "Shangri-La" after the Shangri-La Hotel and Resort, which is set amid 15 acres of exotic gardens, in Singapore.

The Bakers had lived across the street from the hotel with its lush settings while in Singapore – thus the choice of the name "Shangri-La" for their Louisiana mansion. When Baker looks out on his backyard, he loves to point out the wild ducks and other wildlife. He says, "a ready resting place for a man who has found his peace."

16

Mohole

The Mohorovičić Discontinuity, nicknamed Mohole, is the area separating the earth's crust from the upper mantle rock. What is mantle rock? Many people imagine a thick zone of molten magma, since that's what we see coming from volcanoes, but the reality is different. The mantle isn't so much a liquid, like lava or magma, but more like a plastic—solid, but it can move, flow very slowly, and bend. The extreme heat and pressure combine to make the main minerals of the mantle, thought to be olivine (or peridotite), and undergo convection, in which hotter and lighter material rises in plumes toward the crust, while cooler and denser material sinks. There is little data of its geological nature. The mantle makes up about 84 percent of the earth by volume, but its thickness is only about 40 percent of the earth's radius.

The 1,800-mile-thick mantle sits—or more accurately, heaves up and down—just below the earth's crust and above the earth's core. The crust is just a tiny portion of the planet—averaging three to twenty-five miles thick.

In 1957, Walter Munk, one of the most famous oceanographers in the world, and Harry Hess, both of Scripps Institution, suggested the idea behind Project Mohole: to drill into the Mohorovičić Discontinuity (Mohole) and obtain a sample of the earth's mantle. It has often been proposed that the ultimate human future lies in space. It has become clear instead that the strange world holding our future, now and forever, is the ocean. We have recently gained the knowledge that most of our water is four billion years old. Deborah Cramer in her groundbreaking book, *Smithsonian Ocean: Our Water Our World*, states,

"All the water we will ever have, it is our water, and it has made our world. Our lives, and the lives of almost all that dwell on earth, depend on the sea."

Mohole represents earth sciences' answer to the space program. The Soviet Union launched *Sputnik 1*, the first artificial satellite, in 1957. All it did was emit pinging sounds, but progress followed quickly, and it started the space race between the Soviet Union and the United States. The death-lock battle between communism and capitalism with potential nuclear annihilation changed to one of globalization. The whole world watched on live television as Neil Armstrong set foot on the moon in 1969. This brought to people everywhere a profound change in perspective. We were in a new world, thinking and living globally.

The first serious ocean drilling plans were concocted by a handful of geoscience grandees in a group called the American Miscellaneous Society (AMSOC). They were an informal group, sometimes referred to as a "drinking club" of scientists formed to consider proposals that fit into no scientific categories. AMSOC had no officers, no dues, and no bylaws. It was known as a government-funded agency with a sense of humor. Walter Munk describes the American Miscellaneous Society for "maintaining cooperation with visitors from outer space and for informing animals of their proper taxonomic positions." Up until the Mohole Project, 90 percent of the oceanographic research had been funded by the U.S. Navy.

In early 1958, the National Science Foundation agreed to provide $15,000 in initial funds for the project. The National Academy of Sciences became the sponsor of Project Mohole when, in April 1958 with academy assent, the AMSOC Committee of 14 was made a full-fledged unit of the Division of Earth Sciences of the National Research Council, the academy's operating arm. By 1961, they had drilled into the seafloor off the Pacific coast of Baja California. The expedition was the initial phase of a project intended to punch through Earth's crust and reach the underlying mantle. It was called the Mohole Project.

AMSOC contracted with Global Marine of Los Angeles, California, for the use of its oil barge vessel *CUSS I*. The name stood for a consortium of Continental, Union, Superior, and Shell Oil companies. After initial experimentation in 1961, AMSOC brought in Dr. Hollis Hedberg to chair the research group. Hedberg had a record as one of the living legends in the oil business: he was a vice president for exploration worldwide of Gulf Oil (now Chevron) and a professor of geology at Princeton University. Hedberg argued for drilling in the sediments and not spending the money for a big submersible rig to attempt to go to Mohole. Geologists interested in ocean sediments began advocating for a drilling program that would provide several samples of the sedimentary column from a variety of different sites to trace the history of the ocean basins and to determine why the ocean sediments were so much thinner than predicted. Hedberg's group lost the battle.

The Scripps Institution of Oceanography was named for the Scripps family, who were founders of the E.W. Scripps media empire, led by Edward Willis Scripps in 1878. Elizabeth Browning Scripps, his half-sister, joined him at the company and became a major shareholder of the company. She funded the founding of the Scripps Institution of Oceanography in 1903.

The Scripps family trust took control of the Scripps's businesses in 1922 and has overseen it ever since. In 2015, *Forbes* magazine valued the family trust at $7.5 billion. The trust ended in 2012 with the death (at the age of ninety-four) of grandson Robert P. Scripps, who had settled in Fredericksburg, Texas, after serving in the U.S. Army during World War II. In the 1970's he led his family to help create the Robert Paine Scripps Forum for Science, a 16,500-square-foot architectural award–winning oceanfront facility. He also actively supported the Birch Aquarium at Scripps's educational programs connecting children to the world of science.

17
Brown & Root Awarded Contract

The National Science Foundation (NSF) was impressed with the work done in Phase I of the Mohole Project with drilling from the drill barge *CUSS I*. NSF was begun in 1950 with an act of the U.S. Congress, and signed into law by President Harry Truman. The Foundation reports directly to the President, who appoints the NSF Director. NSF is the only U.S. government agency dedicated to supporting basic research and education in all fields of science and engineering.

But NSF felt the AMSOC committee should not manage the Mohole Project's next phases. The NSF solicited bids for Phase II. The bid that had the best evaluation was the one submitted by Socony Mobil (ExxonMobil) with General Motors, Texas Instruments, and Standard of California (Chevron) as partners. In second place was Global Marine with Shell, followed by a bid by Zapata Off-Shore, led then by George H. W. Bush, and partners Dresser Industries and General Dynamics.

The House Appropriations Committee, led by Albert Thomas from Houston, a close friend to George Brown, chose Brown & Root for the contract, which obviously created quite a stir among the oceanographers and in the oil industry. In February 1962, the NSF announced that Brown & Root of Houston would be the prime contractor.

In the second phase, numerous battles started among the scientists, who were split on the direction of the project and how to proceed. Some thought it was becoming a big engineering stunt. Some thought that spending all this money on Mohole would deplete any money for other projects. Most the science community wanted to go for broke and drill a five-mile-deep hole to the Mohole. There were powerful people in the oil industry who preferred a smaller drillship for shallower drilling in the sediments, rather than a big rig designed to drill to the earth's mantle. One of the leading scientists promoting deepwater ocean research was Cesare Emiliani. He was incensed that money was being poured into what he perceived to be an impractical project. He turned out to be right. Emiliani felt it made good sense to drill many boreholes into the ocean sediment to obtain core samples, as opposed to drilling a single hole into the Mohole.

William M. Rice was named director of Project Mohole, and W. H. Tonking was named the deputy manager. Tonking had been recruited by Brown & Root. He assembled a staff of about one hundred and fifty experienced professionals and served as a principal witness at congressional hearings concerning the multibillion-dollar Mohole Project. He negotiated more than a hundred subcontracts with major U.S. firms for sophisticated systems and engineering designs and with construction companies producing major components for the Mohole Project. In 1965, Rice was selected to serve

Paul A. Mattingly Jr.

as chairman of the Deep Drilling Technology Section of the International Upper Mantle Project Symposium held in Ottawa, Canada. The next year, he was awarded the Silver Medal from the Royal Society of Arts in London for his work on the Mohole Project.

18

Mohole Is No Hole

When it was decided to "shoot for the moon" and drill down to the Mohole, the project team recommended that a new vessel be designed and constructed to conduct this experiment under the oceans of Hawaii. At the time, the Russians had announced a similar program to drill deep into the earth. In a sense, it became another Space Race between the Soviets and the United States. However, it wasn't until 1970, when the Russians started drilling Kola SG-3, an exploration well, that after nineteen years of continuous drilling, they reached a staggering world-record depth of 40,230 feet on land.

In 1965, Brown & Root received several bids for the construction of a drilling platform to drill to the Mohole. Levingston had a great working relationship with Brown & Root and hoped to get the contract. But the National Steel and Shipbuilding Company in San Diego bid the contract at a low price and won the job. National Steel had four owners with lots of political influence, including Henry J. Kaiser and Morrison Knudsen. Construction began on the semi-submersible drilling rig that was planned to drill the Mohole. However, the political winds shifted against the project and its large cost. Early mistakes and fumbles about responsibilities for oversight, funding, management, science operations, and scientific advice were corrected. Congress terminated the project a few years later. After spending over an estimated $35 million, the construction of a semi-submersible drilling rig for Mohole at the San Diego shipyard was subsequently halted.

Cancellation of the project was a bitter disappointment for Brown & Root. The Mohole Project was started after Brown & Root was approached by Halliburton Company, an oilfield services business that bought companies with expertise in the oil and gas field. The Halliburton deal was finalized shortly after Brown's death in 1962. It was later merged in with Kellogg Construction and renamed KBR. Recently the Brown & Root brand came back to private ownership when KBR sold the industrial services to form Brown & Root Industrial Service and moved to Baton Rouge, employing six thousand people in the United States, Mexico, and Canada. Jim Bernhard, Jr., of Baton Rouge bought the new firm.

The lessons of Mohole were a warning to scientists to become organized in managing "big science" research. The history exemplifies how not to handle a potentially valuable research program. The hole in the Mohole was fundamentally the fault of the scientists themselves. They did not commit to properly managing the project. It was unheard of for Congress to cancel a project in midstream. But with the escalation of the Vietnam War and attacks led by Congressman Donald Rumsfeld, the project was doomed. Rumsfeld, a young Republican congressman from Illinois, launched a vicious series of attacks against the Mohole. He saw it as a boondoggle for President Lyndon Johnson's longtime supporters, the Brown family, founders of Brown & Root.

By JAMES J. KILPATRICK conservative syndicated columnist.
"The National Science Foundation, chief sponsor of Mohole, made an absurd original estimate of $15 million to complete the work. It was a mistake that cost the sponsors dearly, for the NSF kept having to come back for more money - and more, and more. By the end of the last fiscal year, Congress had funded Mohole to the tune of $55 million, but some estimates placed the final cost at double that sum. THE FOUNDATION erred not only in its wobbly figures, but also in its weak presentation of a case for keeping Mohole alive. Dr. Leland J. Haworth, NSF director, made a poor impression on the Appropriations Committee: "I have lost more sleep in the last three years over the question of what we should do about this project than all the rest of them put together." It was small wonder that the committee decided to give Dr. Haworth a good night's rest. In any event, the $19.7 million asked for fiscal 1967 to continue Project Mohole has now been finally deleted from the budget. The Foundation faces the disheartening task of cancelling 45

contracts, disbanding whole teams of scientists and marine engineers, and halting the construction of the Mohole platform. Last March, it was estimated that cancellation costs would come to $8.2 million, on top of the $16.5 million that had been spent at that time, but these figures are badly out of date. By the time the last settlement is made and the last plans interred in the files, probably $33 million will have gone down the drain. It is hard to be critical of House members who led the light to put an end Mohole. Their one decisive argument was based upon economy. In a time of deficit spending, with costs of Viet Nam constantly mounting, perhaps this costly investment in non-military research should have been suspended. One might wish that these impulses toward economy struck the House more often. * * * YET IT is a pity to see the venture so abruptly abandoned. Granted, Project Mohole was conceived primarily for purposes of pure research. No one knows what lies under the crust of the earth. Core samples from this incredible hole would provide the raw meat that geophysicists feed on. But it was understood, all along, that Mohole would have an immensely valuable spin-off in the development of drilling equipment."

The Mohole Project is a classic example of an optimistic dream that lacked basic skepticism. The technology was not available to carry out the dream. The primary challenges in ultra-deep drilling are temperatures greater than 400° F up to an estimated 1,000° F and high pressures greater than 20,000 psi. The estimated depth to reach the Mohole from sea level is about seven miles. To drill down and access the mantle has remained a dream. The estimated cost is slightly above $1 billion.

One scientist said it is easy to understand why the public was excited about NASA exploring the heavens. But why would we want to explore the oceans and down under? Who wants to explore hell and disturb the devil? Nothing is more evil than the devil.

In Greek mythology, Hades is the brother of Zeus and Poseidon. They all three drew lots to share the universe. Zeus won the heavens; Poseidon, the oceans. Hades drew poorly, which resulted in his becoming lord of the underworld. Besides being called Hades, another name for the underworld is Hell. A certain segment of Americans believes in the devil, and the devil is down below in Hell/Hades!

By 1964, the ASMOC, the original Mohole group of scientists who started the project, disbanded, and the project was left with inadequate scientific support. Shortly thereafter, the same group started the Joint Oceanographic Institutions for Deep Earth Sampling (JOIDES). The membership consisted of scientists from Columbia University's Lamont-Doherty Geological Observatory, the University of Miami's Rosenstein School of Marine and Atmospheric Science, Woods Hole Oceanographic Institution, and the University of California's Scripps Institution of Oceanography. The Deep-Sea Drilling Project (DSDP), as it was called, became a national effort to explore the worldwide geological and geophysical structure of the seafloor through a long-term systematic program that in many ways is ongoing. It was entirely independent from the Mohole Project. Scripps handled the partnership of the institutions. This was a first for oceanography research institutions joining together in any type of research venture. The national Science Foundation felt it had been badly burned by the Mohole fiasco and would only fund the DSDP project for four hundred days, and grant no money for the design and building of any drilling vessels. JOIDES knew that dynamic positioning would be necessary and was being developed in the Mohole Project. However, they knew that drilling would have to be limited to soft semi consolidated sediments, since drilling bits would not be able to be replaced.

Not until the *Glomar Challenger* was operating off the East Coast in 1970 was the technology, created to replace worn drill bits, available on a vessel. From this point, the technology was there to drill deep beneath the oceans, even in hard rock. The drill string of pipe is a hollow through which seawater, the drilling fluid, is pumped down to lubricate the drill bit and clean cuttings from the borehole. In offshore drilling, without a riser, the cuttings are left on the seafloor. But if there is a riser, the fluids are moved back up from the sea floor to the mobile offshore drilling unit (MODU) on the surface.

In 1972, the JOIDES group had added the countries of Russia, Germany, the UK, France, and Japan. In 1973, the White House requested that JOIDES expel Russia from the group, which it did. The legacy of the original group (JOIDES), which had formed in 1964, evolved into the Consortium for Ocean Leadership in 2007. This alliance represents a critical move toward a unified voice in the nation's capital for oceanographic research.

The Consortium for Ocean Leadership is a Washington, DC-based nonprofit organization that represents more than one hundred of the leading public and private ocean research and education institutions, aquariums, and industries with the mission to advance research, education, and sound ocean policy. The DSDP had the scientific and financial backing, but needed a research vessel. In June 1966, the NSF signed a contract with the Scripps Institution for Phase I of the project. On the date of the contract signing, physicist Dr. William Aaron Nierenberg, director of Scripps Institution, announced that a subcontract was let to Global Marine (*Glomar*) to design, build, and operate the drilling operations. Global Marine immediately gave a contract to Levingston to build the vessel. The following year, Phase II of the contract was awarded to the Scripps Institution by the NSF. The amount of the contract was $12.5 million for eighteen months of deep-sea drilling. Global Marine paid Levingston for the *Challenger* drillship with its own money, with the hope that the contract would be extended beyond eighteen months. It was extended for an additional thirty-six months.

The construction of the *Glomar Challenger* drillship raised a lot of questions. How was it going to dig beneath the blue ocean that nobody's ever seen, and discover things about our planet? Scientists had questions such as whether continents move, and what the climate had been like. One of the hopes was to look for life hidden underground, and to try to solve the mystery of the origin of life. The things found from the digs will be a precious record of past changes in the earth's climate.

As the first scientific drillship in human history to drill the oceans of the world, *Glomar Challenger* would capture the imagination of earth scientists throughout the world like the Jules Verne's classic science fiction novel *A Journey to the Centre of the Earth,* penned in 1864. However, the ship would only have five miles of pipe to drill with while the center of the earth was 3,940 miles away.

19
Scripps and Levingston

The tale of Levingston and the earth's secrets started out with a phone call in 1948 from a representative at the Scripps Institution of Oceanography to Willie Ulcher, Levingston's chief engineer at the time. The U.S. Navy was offering Scripps one of the wartime-era ocean rescue tugs - ATA - designed and built by Levingston. Ulcher was the marine engineer who designed this class of tugboats and offered to fly out to San Diego, along with the blueprints, in Levingston's new twin-engine Beechcraft airplane, to discuss the conversion of the tug to a research vessel. My father flew with Ulcher for the meeting. The *ATA-180* was launched July 14, 1944, at the Levingston Shipyard and served in the Asiatic-Pacific Theater. As a tug, the ship had an obscure history, without an entry in the *Dictionary of American Naval Fighting Ships* and only the bare facts of her construction and deployment are known.

The ship became notable in her second career as one of the trailblazing, postwar oceanographic research vessels beginning with her conversion in 1949. Renamed *R/V*

Horizon, she became the vessel enabling Scripps Institution of Oceanography to expand their ocean research from California coastal waters to the blue waters of the global oceans, logging over 610,000 miles. *Horizon* made the first of Scripps's deep sea expeditions, a joint Scripps Institution of Oceanography–U.S. Navy effort in 1950 given the name Midpac, during which it was discovered that the sea floor was young. This discovery changed the conception that the sea floor was old and sediment filled. It established an early lead to the current plate tectonics theory. Plate tectonics is the unifying theory of Earth science and explains many of the major features of how our planet operates. It accounts for Earth's history including the distribution of life and past climate change.

Horizon was one of eighty-nine ATA tugs designed by Levingston and built by the end of WWII. Gulfport Shipbuilding in Port Arthur, Texas, built twenty-two of the ATAs. One of them was given to the Coast Guard for search and rescue. It is called the *WMEC 202 Comanche* museum ship. The *Comanche* is the only Coast Guard-recognized historic nonprofit public accessible Medium Endurance Cutter on the West Coast. The *Comanche* 202 Foundation owns it. While well-worn and aged, the historic World War II-era tug *USCGC Comanche* (ATA-202) is a floating historical museum kept alive by the loving touch of restoration by a team of volunteers. In the Seattle area is another ATA-194 built by Levingston Shipbuilding that has been modified into a luxury fishing yacht. It is named *MODOC*.

Roger Revelle provided a classic definition of good research: "It will be fun to carry out." He was the major proponent of the founding of the University of California, San Diego, in 1960, and the first of its colleges was named in his honor. Revelle was one of the first scientists to study global warming and the movement of earth's tectonic plates. Revelle arranged for the first measurements of atmospheric carbon dioxide by Charles David Keeling, a chemist who joined the SIO staff in 1957.

He was a young PhD from Caltech who was working on measuring CO_2. In March 1958, U.S. climate scientist Charles Keeling began measuring atmospheric CO_2 at the Mauna Loa observatory in Hawaii for use in climate modeling. The first year, 1958, he measured around 315 ppm of carbon dioxide. The measurements have been continuing to this day, managed by his son. They have topped 400 ppm in 2016. It is nicknamed "The Keeling Curve" and made Scripps famous for alerting the world of climate change. In 1977 the U.S. National Academy of Sciences issued the report "Energy and Climate" concluding that the burning of fossil fuels was increasing atmospheric CO_2, and that increased CO_2 was associated with a rise in global temperatures. Revelle is credited with being the godfather of Climate Change due to an article written with Dr. Hans Seuss about increasing CO_2, the oceans, and warming (1957). This is the first shot in the debate over climate change. Oceanographers had believed that the oceans would absorb the excess heat from the CO_2 greenhouse gases. Revelle was one who questioned this thought. It was no secret that the main reservoir of CO_2 was the oceans. Greenhouse gases reflect the solar heat and the oceans are the balancing absorber of the heat. How much and what will the oceans do with the heat is a complex question of which the climate change scientists are seriously trying to find answers. Deniers of climate change today often repeat the myths that because carbon dioxide is invisible and only a trace gas, it can't possibly cause significant climate change.

In his recent book, Thomas L. Friedman, a New York Times op-ed columnist, writes about foreign affairs, globalization, and technology in his book *Thank You for Being Late*. Friedman says that the biggest forces reshaping more things in more ways on more days are accelerations in technology, globalization, and climate change.

There is no debate whether fossil fuel burning creates CO_2 and is a factor in adding to the greenhouse gases reflecting heat back down to earth. The debate is mainly around what impact the heat has on Earth. However, some of the heat created is natural. The climate science experts tell us that the additional heat reflected by greenhouse gases is being caused by humans. This is a simple thing, although complex in their actual actions. One key fact is that if we didn't have greenhouse gases the earth would be cold. An estimated zero degrees.

The great debate is simply the warming of Earth. What we have are the fossils and the mud (sediments) of geology to give us history. The core samples, beginning with the *Glomar Challenger* scientific drillship, started the legacy of unbelievable data that is continuing with the IODP program.

From a lecture series by the famous scientist, Richard P. Feynman discussing the key to science: *If it disagrees with experiment, it's wrong. In that simple statement is the key to science. It doesn't make any difference how beautiful your guess is, it doesn't matter how smart you are who made the guess, or what his name is ... If it disagrees with experiment, it's wrong. That's all there is to it.*

20

From Ashes of Disaster Grow the Roses of Success

Levingston and Global Marine had wanted to build a rig for scientific ocean drilling. They were disappointed when the initial contract for a semisubmersible rig was given to a San Diego shipyard in 1964 to drill the Mohole. Now with that deal terminated, the opportunity arose to build a state-of-the-art drillship for the next big project.

The building of the *Glomar Challenger* is a story of getting the "cowboys, engineers, software pioneers and geoscientists working together," designing and building a remarkable tool for deep ocean scientific exploration. Experts from science, government, and the oil industry set aside their differences. New technology allowed them to do things that previously were unattainable. It turned out to be a ship that was going to mean something to the world.

Levingston laid the keel of the R/V *Glomar Challenger* on October 18, 1967. On March 23, 1968, "with a bottle of seawater mixed from the Atlantic and Pacific Oceans, symbolic of the far-flung operations scheduled for the scientific program,"

Edith Meyerson Nierenberg (Mrs. William A. Nierenberg) christened the *Glomar Challenger* at the Levingston shipyard in Orange, Texas. Nierenberg was the chancellor for Scripps beginning in 1965.

Scripps Institution of Oceanography and the William A. Nierenberg family honored ocean frontier explorer and Academy Award winning filmmaker, James Cameron, with the 12th annual 2013 Nierenberg Prize for Science in Public Interest. Cameron first found major success with the science fiction action film *The Terminator* (1984) and the epic movie *Titanic* (1997). Cameron has been on the advisory board of Scripps Institution of Oceanography since 2002. On March 26, 2012, Cameron piloted the craft, *Deepsea Challenger*, a 24-ft. submersible, in reaching the bottom of Challenger Deep, the deepest point on Earth.

The newly christened, *Glomar Challenger*, smoothly glided into the Sabine River, from the Levingston Shipyard in Orange, Texas. This marked the historical beginning for the *Challenger*, a name proposed by Dr. T. H. van Adel, a well-known research geologist. At the time, a lot of reputations were on the line with this ship and its mission. Many engineers and scientists thought it would be another disaster like the Mohole project. A great deal of thought and hard work had gone into the *Challenger* project, going back to that famous breakfast in April 1957 on Walter Munk's patio, when a group of scientists decided to attempt to do research on the earth's inner space.

The Mohole's successor program had much more modest and achievable goals that kept the scientific community excited and engaged as remarkable discoveries were made in every ocean basin. They needed a special-purpose ship to probe the bottoms of the oceans. There was talk of naming the ship *Phoenix,* after the mythical bird that emerged from the ashes of its predecessor. The most important thing that the scientists had going for them was the support and cooperation of the oil industry. Without the industry's support, the design and construction of the research vessel would have been impossible. The National Science Foundation committed to $7.5 million for eighteen months. Global Marine had to pay for the *Glomar Challenger.* If not for the oil industry, the project wouldn't have been done.

The first leg, led by Maurice "Doc" Ewing, drilled into the cap rock of a salt dome in the Gulf of Mexico in 11,719 feet of water, where geophysical evidence suggested the crust might be oceanic, rather than continental. Ewing had been a major cheerleader for the drilling of a deep hole. Some regarded it as impractical or wild. True, it was not practical or it couldn't have been done. But the offshore oil industry was turning the corner developing the knowledge. The *Glomar Challenger* was fortunate to be led by Ewing on the original voyage of the drilling program. He was a hands-on guy who wanted to be where the action was. His outstanding contributions to geophysics were recognized by the conferring of eleven honorary degrees by universities in the United States and four foreign countries. He was also awarded fifteen medals and prizes, including the National Medal of Science, the Vetlsen Award of Columbia University, the Navy's Distinguished Service Award, the Gold Medal of the Royal Astronomical Society, the Agassiz Medal of the National Academy of Science, the Medal of Honor from Rice University, the Wollaston Medal of the Geological Society of London, the Day Medal and Penrose Medal of the Geological Society of America, the Bowie Medal of the American Geophysical Union, and the Sidney Powers Medal of the American Association of Petroleum Geologists. In 1976 the Geophysics Laboratory of the University of Texas Marine Science Institute was renamed Maurice Ewing Hall. Dr. John Anderson is the current Maurice Ewing Professor of oceanography at Rice University.

Scientists ran the *Glomar Challenger* purely for earth science research. As of 2014, The Integrated Ocean Deepwater Program (IODP) had twenty-one countries contributing, with the United States and Japan as the leading participants. The coordinated use of core samples, drillships, and mission-specific platforms has resulted in a community and facility-oriented approach and a concentration of effort by a diverse group of scientists. All parts of the Earth system are linked through flows of mass, energy, and life. Buried beneath the ocean floor are records of millions of years of Earth's climatic, biological, chemical, and geological history.

Who Is Involved in IODP?

IODP is funded by four entities acting as international partners:

> The U.S. National Science Foundation (NSF) and Japan's Ministry of Education, Culture, Sports, Science, and Technology (MEXT) are Lead Agencies.

The European Consortium for Ocean Research Drilling (ECORD) is a Contributing Member.

The People's Republic of China Ministry of Science and Technology (MOST) is an Associate Member.

Interim Asian Consortium, represented by the Korea Institute of Geoscience and Mineral Resources (KIGAM), is an Associate Member.

"The IODP is a historical milestone with cooperation among nations, not for political or military might but for the benefit of all humankind. Not only do we have the IODP program, but we have numerous other ocean research legacies such as the Eric and Wendy Schmidt establishment of the Schmidt Ocean Institute in 2009 as a seagoing research facility, as well. Its mission is as follows: combine advanced science with state-of-the-art technology to achieve lasting results in ocean research, to catalyze sharing of the information, and to communicate this knowledge to audiences around the world. We foster a deeper understanding of our environment." Source: The IODP.

Two events in 1968 saw dramatic milestones in scientific exploration. The first milestone, on August 11, 1968, was the *Glomar Challenger* sailing down the Sabine River to the Gulf of Mexico from the Levingston Shipyard in Orange, Texas. This began the deepwater drilling project (DSDP) that is carried on to this day. The second of two milestones was on December 21, 1968, with the launch of *Apollo 8*. It was the first manned space flight to the moon. Astronauts, Frank Borman, Jim Lovell, and Bill Anders became the first humans to orbit another world.

Why should we explore the ocean bottoms and below it? Because it is part of the "final frontier." It is 3,950 miles to the center of the earth and the deepest we have drilled is only 8 miles. People think that we've explored the Earth—that we're done. "Let's go to Mars. Let's check out other planets." Yet our lives are dependent on our oceans and earth. Today, we are barely touching the earth sciences and how our oceans impact our lives. Oceans are a critical player in the basic elements we need to survive. Ocean plants produce half of the world's oxygen, and these amazing waters absorb nearly one-third of human-caused carbon dioxide emissions. Oceans also regulate our weather and form the clouds that bring us fresh water.

21

Inward-Looking Telescope

Glomar Challenger was to the earth science community what the telescope was to astronomers. The *Challenger* drillship became an inward-looking telescope that revolutionized the way we think about the earth, almost as completely and as quickly as Galileo changed our view of the solar system in 1610 when he first saw moons revolving around Jupiter. The drillship opened a whole new world of scientific exploration prospects. It enabled research of fundamental problems that were completely unavailable from any other method. As the twentieth-century German dramatist Bertolt Brecht, who wrote the play *Life of Galileo,* put it: "Astronomy did not progress for one thousand years because astronomers did not have a telescope."

In 1970, Arthur Maxwell, Richard Von Herten, K. J. Hsu, James Andrews, Tsunamis Saito, Stephen F. Percival Jr., E. D. Milow, and Robert Boyce reported on the eighteen-month South Atlantic Ocean cruise of the *Glomar Challenger* for the Joint Oceanographic Institutions for Deep Earth Sampling. Their findings provided conclusive evidence confirming the global hypotheses of seafloor spreading and continental drift and signaled the arrival of a new era in geologic research—global plate tectonics. It was later determined that the birth of the Atlantic likely began forming about 200 million years ago.

Scientists now tell us that the earth was once one big supercontinent named Pangea surrounded by one global ocean. The continent did not last. About 250 million years ago, it started ripping apart up into smaller continents moving to their present places, becoming today's continents.

Pangea's existence was first proposed in 1912 by German meteorologist, Alfred Wegener, as a part of his theory of continental drift. Its name is derived from the Greek *Pangaea*, meaning "all the earth." Continental drift explained why continents' shapes fit together like pieces of a puzzle and why distant continents had the same fossils. Wegener wrote a book explaining his idea called *The Origins of Continents and Oceans*. Geologists almost universally rejected it. The mechanism for the breakup of Pangea is now explained in terms of plate tectonics, rather than Wegener's outmoded concept of continental drift.

We now know that, directly or indirectly, plate tectonics influences nearly all geologic processes, past and present. Indeed, the notion that the entire Earth's surface is continually shifting has profoundly changed the way we view our world.

One of the geologists, Dr. Edward "Jerry" Winterer, Scripps distinguished research professor who worked on the *Glomar Challenger*, said in 2006, "We began to understand the oceans and their history in a way that was totally out of reach before…the layers beneath the bottom of the sea, more than, let's say ten meters down beneath the mud, were inaccessible to us without drilling. And so, we figured out how to drill into the sediments, distances of two kilometers into it, in water depths of several kilometers, so that the ocean basins became essentially accessible to us clear down to the beginning of its history." He continued, "With the deep-sea drilling program, we can reconstruct ocean history back about 150 million years and learn the states of the ocean and the circulation pattern and how it was." Winterer once claimed that the *"Glomar Challenger* unlocks the earth's mysteries." And it did!"

The research has gone on and the geological record contains numerous periods when abrupt increases in CO_2 coincided with ocean acidification for the presence, during past events, of changes and warming. The deep-sea core geologic record allows us to look at the changes predicted by experiments. For example, an event 55 million years ago, included a massive carbon release (3-6 trillion tons) caused by methane hydrate that caused ocean acidification and global warming. Valuable lessons are being learned about how marine life adjusts to climate change.

It wasn't until the *Glomar Challenger* that evidence was gathered showing that continents do indeed move. Plate tectonics revolutionizes earth sciences by providing the fundamental mechanism by which the planet surfaces operated with implication for mountain building, climate, and the origin of life on earth. This created excitement and chaos, opening opportunities for young scientists to get in on the ground floor of the scientific revolution. The excitement spread all over the world, as young people wanted to get in on the new thing. From the study of rocks, geology expanded to what is called geoscience, broadening our knowledge of Earth and planetary systems, and providing solutions to pressing societal problems, including reliable and affordable energy future. The science has diversified into specialties covering a broad range of opportunities.

The book that best captures the historical significance of the *Glomar Challenger* is: *A Ship That Revolutionized Earth Science* Kenneth Jinghwa Hsu originally published in 1992. Princeton University Press.

> *"The famous geological research ship Glomar Challenger was a radically new instrument that revolutionized earth science in the same sense that the cyclotron revolutionized nuclear physics, and its deep-sea drilling voyages, conducted from 1968 through 1983, were some of the great scientific adventures of our time. Beginning with the vessel's first cruises, which lent support to the idea of continental drift, the Challenger played a key part in the widely-publicized plate-tectonics revolution and its challenge to more conventional theories."*

Since its founding in 1869, the American Museum of Natural History in New York City has been a world leader in the natural sciences. David S. and Ruth L. Gottesman Hall of Planet Earth, located in the Rose Center for Earth and Space, has a fabulous section titled, "Why Are Ocean Basins, Continents, and Mountains?" It covers earthquakes and plate tectonics and states: "Most earthquakes occur at plate boundaries. Where plates spread apart, earthquakes are shallow and small. Where plates slip past each other, they are shallow but frequently large. The San Andreas Fault (California) 753 miles long, is one such boundary. Where plates collide, earthquakes mark zones where one plate dives beneath another. These earthquakes occur at various depths, from shallow to deep."

What drives the movement of the plates? The basic concept is that heat inside the earth rises and drives the movement of the continents/plates. The source of heat driving the convection currents is radioactivity deep in the Earth's mantle.

Why do earthquakes occur? Earthquakes occur because the Earth's plates are in motion. As transform faults were being discovered, oceanographers prepared for the most intensive sampling of the sea floor ever undertaken using the research vessel the, *Glomar Challenger*. In 1968, drill cores showed that the sea floor grows older with distance from the mid-ocean ridges. Together with the magnetic data and transform faults, the cores indicated sea floor spreading must take place. Suddenly, scientists could easily explain many aspects of Earth's geology and history which had long been unclear. Not only could the distribution of fossils and paleoclimates be explained, but the origins of mountain ranges, mineral resources, large faults, and magnetic field patterns also made sense. Core samples are a treasure trove for understanding how Earth's climate and life evolved. The geologic record is the best source to a controlled experiment.

The *Glomar Challenger* was given its name as a tribute to the accomplishments of a nineteenth-century oceanographic survey vessel, the HMS *Challenger*. From 1872 to 1896, it traveled across the world over 70,000 miles to survey the ocean floor in the world's first major oceanographic project that helped established oceanography as a science. The name of the ship has a story to it as well. Glomar is a truncation of "global marine." When the deep-water drilling group contacted the British government for usage of the *Challenger* name, they were referred to the British scientific community. That group enthusiastically gave the okay to name the American ship after their HMS *Challenger*. The British had never allowed it to be used by a foreign country until then. To seal the deal, British scientists gave a few artifacts from the HMS *Challenger* to put on board the *Glomar Challenger*. The scientific mission of the *Glomar Challenger* put it in a small, elite group of ships that had conducted oceanic research. In total, the *Glomar Challenger* represented a combination of advanced technologies primarily from the oil and gas industry. It was a testimonial to Levingston's and Global Marine's engineering, design, and remarkable fabrication efforts.

Hayes B. Jacobs, a famous nonfiction writer, described the moon pool in an article titled *Voyage of the Glomar Challenger* in the Standard Oil of New Jersey (ExxonMobil) publication, 1969, for shareholders and employees:

"Had he boarded the *Glomar Challenger*, he would have been even more puzzled on seeing that the tower stands athwart a huge hole, amidships, a twenty-by-twenty-two-foot aperture that led one observer to call the ship "a floating donut." In the same article, Jacobs wrote, "Acclaim for the project (*Glomar Challenger*) is widespread."

Dr. Howard R. Gould, research scientist with Esso Production Research Company, and that company's coordinator with the project, calls the program "probably the most important geological research project of this century." Such systematic study, he feels, is ending a "guessing game" regarding the origin, age, and history of the oceans' basins—a subject that has long intrigued earth scientists. The story in *The LAMP* shows the total support of the oil industry for the *Glomar Challenger* scientific expedition. Standard Oil hired a big-name artist to paint a full-page picture of the *Glomar Challenger*. Without the technological, personnel, and moral support of the oil industry, it could not have happened. This is a classic example of what can happen when industry, academia, and government work closely together on a project.

These ships were the beginning of advanced drillship designs, with probably the key technology being the *Challenger*'s dynamic positioning system with acoustic sensors, which was also the key technology for the *Explorer*. At the time, the *Glomar Challenger* was the only drillship capable of drilling in three to four miles of water depth. Parts of the *Glomar Challenger*, such as its dynamic positioning system, engine telegraph, and thruster console, are stored at the Smithsonian Institution. After ninety-six voyages and six hundred drilling sites, the *Glomar Challenger* tied dock for the last time with the Deep-Sea Drilling Project in November 1983.

The *Glomar Challenger* was replaced with an oil drillship renamed the *JOIDES Resolution* (*JR*) and modified to be a seagoing research vessel. Why "*JOIDES Resolution*"? The research vessel is named for HMS *Resolution*, commanded by Captain James Cook more than two hundred years ago, which explored the Pacific Ocean, its islands, and the Antarctic region.

Also in 1983, the management of the ocean-drilling program was moved from Scripps to Texas A&M University, the second-most highly funded research program in Texas after the Johnson Space Center (NASA). The university had built a fifteen-story oceanography building next to the main building at the College Station campus. Referred to as the O&M (Oceanography and Meteorology) Building around campus, it opened in 1972 and is the tallest building at Texas A&M. The 109,609 square feet of the O&M Building are filled with offices, classrooms, labs, and storage space. James Earl Rudder, the President of Texas A&M (1959 – 1970), was a visionary leader determined to get into the earth sciences and oceanography in a big way. Money was short, but he found a big resource in the federal government.

Texas A&M Oceanography Building

Today, the Texas A&M Geoscience VISION statement says, "We will lead in establishing the geosciences as the defining scientific discipline of the twenty-first century. We know that the sustainable human society of the future depends more on innovation and application of discovery in the geosciences than on any other discipline. Therefore, our field is essential to solving society's grand challenges—global climate change, air and water quality, and adequate energy and food supplies."

Off the coast of Guatemala during an expedition in 1981, the *Glomar Challenger* scientists recovered the first sample of methane gas hydrates to be studied in a laboratory. Methane is the primary component of natural gas, and methane hydrate is a naturally occurring compound made up of a water/ice cage surrounding a methane molecule. Gas hydrates are naturally occurring and form under specific conditions of low temperature and high pressure. Once it is "melted" or exposed to pressure and temperature conditions which make it unstable, the gas molecule is dissociated or released by the water. This is apparent when putting a lit match to methane hydrate and seeing what appears to be burning ice. In Guatemala, a three-foot length of core was retrieved that contained methane hydrate. The drill cores bubbled and fizzed like a submarine version of a freshly opened soda bottle. "People on the ship didn't know what to make of them," said oceanographer William P. Dillon. They immediately shipped it to the Colorado School of Mines, where it sparked excitement. "It was not until back in the lab, that people thought about them and realized gas hydrates existed in seafloor sediment," Dillon said.

This sample became the impetus for the first national research and development program dedicated to methane hydrates by the United States. This was an incredible story. Over the last thirty years, methane has gone from being a gas of no importance to possibly the most important greenhouse gas both for understanding climate change and as a cost-effective target for future emission reductions and source of energy. Only since 2004 has it become an object of serious consideration as a potential fossil energy source for the future. It is now possible to project the available global amounts with some confidence.

At one time, methane hydrates were joked about. The ice would burn and it was thought to be a novelty—a great trick for a magician's show. It was not even mentioned in the news media. Some estimates have gone as far as to predict that hydrocarbon volumes trapped in gas (methane) hydrates may equal the total equivalent energy resources bound in other conventional hydrocarbon sources such as coal, natural gas, and oil. Gas hydrates may be a significant source of energy if ways can be found to safely exploit them. Despite all the hype, the reality is that the size of the global methane hydrate inventory is unknown. This huge potential, alone, warrants a new look at advanced technologies that might one day be safe and cost-effective in detecting and producing natural gas from methane hydrates.

Yet, it is perceived by some as a danger. Marine sediments suggest that the earth was once a much warmer place - that a massive release of greenhouse gases, yet to be understood, spiked temperatures. The suggested source is methane hydrates.

Further research will provide clues to climate changes from a hot planet to a cold one. The past 56 million years of cores and wireline logs offer some interesting data on warming.

A continuing close partnership with the research groups such as the IODP is necessary to continue to address these challenges. Several studies suggest that as the ocean warms, the hydrates might melt and potentially release methane into the ocean waters and atmosphere. We have come a long way from the days of the *Glomar Challenger* and "fire in the water." It is conceded that there are many unanswered questions in gas hydrate exploration. The most critical challenge of life may be to fully understand the energy resource and environmental implications of naturally occurring gas hydrate. Methane is a greenhouse gas that can remain in the atmosphere for about seven to ten years before it's converted to carbon dioxide, which remains in the atmosphere for over a century. Methane only recently became part of the public consciousness. It is barely known and a reminder that we hardly know our own planet. Gas hydrate—basically methane frozen under high pressures and low temperatures—has potential as a source of abundant energy, if it can be extracted and turned into usable form. It also has potential to do great harm, if global warming results in melting hydrate that releases methane, a powerful greenhouse gas, into the atmosphere.

22
Miracle of the Computer

When the *Glomar Challenger* Project started, the big question was how to keep a ten-thousand-ton ship stationary over a fixed spot on the ocean floor in miles of water, while drilling a hole in the ocean bottom. The solution was a dynamic positioning (DP) system that was the culmination of more than ten years of research with the Mohole Project starting with the *Cuss 1*, a modified barge. The first mention of dynamic positioning was in the famous science fiction writer, Jules Verne's novel, *Propeller Island,* published in 1895. The story is about an artificial movable island, four-miles-long by three-miles-wide, moving around in the Pacific Ocean along the California coast. The island was motorized by millions of horsepower created with steam from burning petroleum briquettes. It produced electric energy and powered hundreds of propellers to move around, going as far as the Hawaiian Islands. An excerpt reads: "Since the self-propelled island needed to remain at a distance from land to keep from running aground, she was not "moored" in the strict sense of the term. In other words, anchors were not used, as this would have been impossible at depths of one hundred meters or more. Thus, by means of the machines, which maneuver ahead and astern throughout its stay, it is kept in place, as immobile as the eight main islands of the Hawaiian Archipelago."

During construction at the Levingston Shipyard, the workers created a term of affection for the software engineers. They were called "thinkers," coined by Penn Johnson, a Levingston engineer, for the team from AC Electronics/Defense Research Laboratories (Delco division of General Motors) Santa Barbara, California, who were building the sophisticated dynamic positioning computer system on the *Glomar Challenger.*

Interestingly, the AC initials stand for AC Sparkplugs founded by Albert Champion. The staff of the AC team were the specialists in research development and production of guidance and navigational and control systems for the Apollo Command and Lunar Module spacecraft in landing men on the moon. America's first team of three astronauts used the system to guide them to the moon and back. Neil Armstrong stepped onto the lunar surface and described the event as, "That's one small step for man, one giant leap for mankind." The date was July 20, 1969.

While installing the digital computer system, the AC Electronics personnel stayed at the Jack Tar hotel across the river from the Livingston Shipyard. The ship was designed and built with marine and petroleum technology from the oil industry. The dynamic positioning technology originated from the federal government and NASA. The concept of software engineering was officially coined in 1968 about the time of the maiden voyage of the *Glomar Challenger*. Yet nobody at Levingston understood the lingo of a software engineer. No one even knew what a software engineer was at the time. Many thought that a software engineer was a fancy name for a file clerk. Salaries for computer programmers did not keep up with the salaries of engineers. Traditional engineers believed that software programming (or coding) was a more menial type of work than traditional engineering. It wasn't until people like Bill Gates, Paul Allen, Larry Ellison, Ross Perot, Steve Jobs, and Steve Wozniak showed the world the importance of software design and development, that it became appreciated.

Thomas R. Stockton, a software engineer, was called in from California when the sea-trials in the Gulf of Mexico for the *Glomar Challenger* met with troubles from the dynamic positioning system. This was the last test before acceptance of the vessel from Levingston. It was costing Global Marine $25,000 a day for reimbursement by the National Science Foundation, which could not start before acceptance of the DP system. The system was flawed in that at a certain point, the computer would turn all the four tunnel thrusters and two stern propellers on full power. The two software engineers from AC Electronics had been working night and day for over a week trying to find the bad code. Global Marine Vice President, Curtis Crooke, was concerned as he counted the money Global Marine was losing due to the delay. Stockton arrived in Galveston and went out on the *Challenger*. After only a few hours, he found the bad code and fixed it. Stockton told me it was easy to fix since he had written the code and knew exactly where to look for the trouble. Scripps accepted the ship on the twenty-third day after leaving port.

Later, Stockton consulted Global Marine Development, Inc. on the *Hughes Glomar Explorer* Deep Sea Mining Program. Stockton was responsible for the technical/schedule/cost monitoring of subcontractors for the electronics, instrumentation, and computer systems. Stockton told me that, looking back, it is amazing what was done with slide rules to make quick calculations of engineering and design. That "manual hand calculator" was sometimes referred to as the "magician's wand." No doubt, the advancement in computer power was "huge."

At the time, Stockton worked for AC Electronics, Delco, the division of General Motors that had the prime contract for the Apollo Guidance System. NASA was also providing funds for the MIT Center for Space Research and contracted with MIT's Instrumentation Laboratory for the development of the Apollo Guidance System.

The software engineering for the *Glomar Challenger* was fundamental in the introduction of software engineering to the oil and gas industry. In 1975, Robert H. Cannon, Jr., emphasized the historical significance of the *Glomar Challenger* in advancing computer technology at a talk titled "Smart Energy: A Key Role for Computers" at Caltech in a Watson Lecture at Beckman Auditorium. "The miracle of the digital computer is giving us the opportunity to employ new levels of care and skill in solving our energy shortage problems.... The computer can do it. ... As we reach farther and farther for our energy resources, we're going to have to operate with machines where men cannot go searching, probing, extracting, and harvesting—all by remote control. The first was the Glomar *Challenger*, a ship designed to drill holes in the bottom of the sea, to learn how the sea floor was formed, to learn more about the plate tectonics puzzle, and to learn where minerals and resources might be. This means controlling, from the surface, a submerged drill string three or four miles long, threading a needle underwater by pushing on the other end of the thread about four miles away."

At the time, Cannon was chairman of Caltech's Division of Engineering and Applied Science. Cannon had done a lot of research himself in such fields as automatic flight and space vehicle control, gyroscopes, and inertial guidance. He got his Sc.D. from MIT in 1950. Cannon said, "The Glomar Challenger team solved this central problem with a sonar sensor on the end of the drill string, and a managing computer to operate the ship so it would move in just the right way to drop the drill string into the hole. Around the hole, there were three sonar reflectors (which produced echoes) on a fifteen-foot cone. The computer compared the three signals to determine where the drill bit was in relation to the hole. The computer on the ship had built into its memory a full understanding of the dynamic response of the ship and its four-mile-long piece of spaghetti, so it could figure out precisely how to move the ship around on the surface."

Important Source: (Cannon, Robert H. Jr. "Smart Energy: A Key Role for Computers," *Engineering and Science* 40: no. 1 [October-November 1976]: 9-12, 28-29, http://calteches.library.caltech.edu/363/1/smart.pdf.)

Initially, chert or flint (hard rock) layers in the deep ocean sediments of the Eocene and older ages, led to the early destruction of milled cutter core bits. During the first several years, twelve different types of drill bits were tried to analyze the best performance. After several years, it was agreed that a tungsten carbide insert roller worked best. To this day, rotary technology is a mechanical grinding process that is limited by rock hardness, deep pressures, and high temperatures. They were faced with the problem to reenter the same hole after they'd broken a drill bit—or after they'd been away for a week, or months. Without this reentry capability, you can drill only as deep as one bit will take you. With reentry, there's no such limit. In 1973, with the use of the reentry cone, they could reenter the borehole in 18,108 feet of water depth. In 1978 they could drill a hole in the Mariana Trench in 23,078 feet of water depth. This was an amazing feat at the time. Scientific deep sea drilling vessel *Chikyu* broke the record in 2012 reaching 25,400 feet.

The desire by scientists to recover a complete, undisturbed section of the uppermost crustal material has required some technological development by the scientific community. The greatest advance in this regard for the recovery of sediments was the development of a hydraulic piston core that can be triggered to shoot out ahead of the drill bit and recover a virtually undisturbed 9 m (29-ft.) section of sediment. For the oil industry, one thing the *Glomar Challenger* proved was that man could drill for oil in the deep waters of the oceans.

John Hogan, a retired engineer from AC Electronics, explained that today, we have more capacity in our laptops than in those old computer systems, such as the one on the *Glomar*

Challenger. The limitations of the old computers forced early computer scientists to be creative. As the number of lines of code increased, so did the number of potential bugs, so keeping the code more compact left less room for hidden errors. The software engineers on the *Glomar Challenger* were forced to be more efficient due to the limitations imposed on the team by the memory technology available. At that time, engineers at AC Electronics were trained for NASA's Apollo mission work, so they needed to reduce lines of code to get the maximum reliability. As Gordon Bell, father of the minicomputer at Digital Equipment Corp (DEC) stated, "The most reliable components are the ones you leave out." AC Electronics culture was tuned with reliability for the Apollo program. After all, a mistake could easily cost the lives of our astronauts. This was important to get right, as the *Challenger* would be working far out in the middle of the ocean. In fact, the designers did not put a heliport on the drillship due to the work locations being out of the range of helicopters.

Instructions would be given to the programs by punch cards. There were no hard disks. All the data was stored on magnetic tape. The programs used were written in Assembly and IBM's Fortran, the first higher-level programming language created in 1957. In May 1962, another milestone was traversed. An ASA committee started developing a standard for the Fortran language, a very important step that made it worthwhile for vendors to produce Fortran systems for every new computer.

W. P. Schneider was a key man in the development of the dynamic positioning system. After graduating from the

University of Houston, Schneider received a full scholarship from the Massachusetts Institute of Technology and was the first U of H graduate to attend MIT. Schneider earned his master's degree in electrical engineering, and then came back to the University of Houston in 1951 as an assistant professor and started working during the summer for Schlumberger. He went from Schlumberger to Brown & Root Inc. of Houston, Texas, as the 'prime contractor for Project Mohole, where he was project engineer for electronics.

Two particularly difficult problems were perfected during the Project Mohole mission phase: (1) how to detect the self-powered beacon located on the ocean floor, despite engine noise, and (2) how to develop the technology to move the ship from side to side while positioning the ship over the drill hole. Schneider recalled: "To stay in the correct position over the drilling site, we had to be able to move the ship sideways, so we installed two computer-controlled thrusters in the stern and two in the bow. We were talking to the Navy, and we were trying to determine the precise amount of thrust we were going to need to move the ship sideways. We had to stay within an area that was roughly the width of the vessel, so we asked them, 'What do we need for the moment of inertia in moving port to starboard?' There was a long silence, and they finally said, 'We don't move our ships that way.'"

How does the dynamic positioning system operate?

At the time, the sky was not full of satellites for Global Positioning Systems (GPS). NASA had six satellites flying over the poles. They were not adequate for keeping a fixed position. Advanced as we are, humans still can't see through water. Sonar is the use of sound waves to find objects under water. Aristotle was one of the first, if not the first, to recognize that sound could be heard in water as well as air. Later, Leonardo da Vinci observed that by placing a long tube in the water and the other end to the ear one could hear ships from afar. Sonar research got going during World War II with the U.S. Navy trying to locate German and Japanese submarines. After the war, the Navy was the major source of funding for oceanography institutions and sonar research was a major focus.

Huffington Post: An Interview with World Renowned Oceanographer - Walter Munk 04/26/2016, January 31, 2016. Max Guinn and Walter Munk, at Munk's home in La Jolla, California. Credit: S. Guinn

Ask my generation—I am 15—to identify its heroes, and you will likely be given a roster of NBA names. Few, if any, have heard of Walter Munk, the world's greatest living oceanographer. Called "The Einstein of the Oceans" by the New York Times, Munk's scientific contributions are almost unbelievable. Following Munk's accomplishments is a Forrest Gump journey through history.

As far as great inventors go, Munk ranks with Thomas Edison. He is recognized for groundbreaking discoveries in wave propagation, ocean drilling, tides, currents, worldwide ocean circulation, and even our understanding of why the moon stopped rotating. His work serves as the basis for deep sea oil drilling and scientific ocean exploration.

Before Walter Munk, deep sea drilling was thought impossible. There was no known method of keeping a drilling ship stationary, as there was

no form of stable measurement or GPS. Munk and his team devised a system using sound for triangulation. The vessel sent and received sound impulses from three transponders on the ocean floor. By measuring the time, it took for the impulses to travel between them, they could calculate the ship's exact location. "That had never been done," Munk told me, "and that was really, tremendously important because it became the basis of deep sea drilling for oil." This work also served as the foundation for drilling in the deep-sea floor for scientific reasons, becoming a major source of geologic research for the last fifty years.

The objective of the *Glomar Challenger's* dynamic positioning system was to keep the ship from moving too far and breaking the drill pipe between the ship and the borehole in the ocean bottom. The pulse signals from the acoustic beacon on the ocean floor transmit to the receiving hydrophones on the bottom of the ship's hull and give the ship's position relative to the beacons. One gyroscopic platform tilt indicator is located near the ship's center. The computer analyzes the data for position, heading, and rate of movement with other data from sensors on wind direction and intensity, currents, ship's pitch, roll and heading, being recorded simultaneously. The computer compares these parameters with the desired ship's position and heading. The computer activates the necessary ship propellers and/or tunnel thrusters. The 59-inch diameter thruster's propellers - of which there were four - deliver up to 18,000 pounds per thrust at Schottel S300 545-rpm cycloidal propellers. The computer system designed for the *Glomar Challenger* used a digitally modified Scientific Data System (SDS) Sigma 2, sixteen-bit, 64k computer. Re-programming could completely change the basic control equations. The "primitive computer," as far as speed and memory are concerned, nevertheless had capacities that are advanced by today's standards.

It is significant that the dynamic positioning computer system automatically controlled the ship's propulsion system to keep the vessel in position without any external human effort. I am told that to use the word "robotics" is not appropriate to describe it, as it implies human effort. Thus, a more proper analogy would be a drone system. Of course, it also had manual and semiautomatic modes of operation.

Collaborating with MIT's Instrumentation Lab was the AC Spark Plug Division of General Motors for fabrication of the inertial, gyroscope-stabilized platform of the Apollo spacecraft, for development and construction of ground support and checkout equipment, and for assembling and testing all parts of the system. A short time later, a contract was given to the AC Spark Plug Division by Brown & Root for the Dynamic Positioning System of the Mohole Project.

23

Hughes Glomar Explorer Inspired by the *Glomar Challenger*

The name *Hughes Glomar Explorer*, to the minds of many, is the most famous built-in-America ship. *Hughes* refers to the famous Howard H. Hughes. The CIA managed to convince the world that billionaire Howard Hughes had decided to invest millions of dollars to scoop up "manganese nodules," balls of heavy metals that lie on the ocean floor. The agency needed to fool not just the world, but a diverse range of special interests: ship-building unions, stockholders, environmental watchdogs, and the media.

    The *Explorer* was also designed by Global Marine and built four years after the *Glomar Challenger*. Like the *Challenger*, it was also a drillship with an automatic digital computer positioning and guidance system, except its mission was to find and retrieve the Russian nuclear missile submarine *K-129*. It should have been called the *Challenger*, and the *Challenger* should have been called the *Explorer*, since its mission was to explore the inner layers of the earth. The *Hughes Glomar Explorer* was built for the CIA with help from the eccentric, reclusive multi-billionaire, Hughes, and was part of the most famous high-sea espionage tale of the cold war—a tale celebrated as one of the greatest covert missions of the CIA.

The cultural effect of *Hughes Glomar Explorer* is indicated by the reference to it in the book *The Hunt for Red October*, which launched Tom Clancy's phenomenal writing career. The movie adaptation, with the same name, starred Sean Connery and Alec Baldwin.

At age eighteen, after the death of his parents, Hughes took over control of the Hughes Tool Company, which practically had a monopoly on oil drilling bits. The Hughes drill bits were critically significant in the growth of the oil industry. The company generated so much cash flow, it enabled the only shareholder, Howard Hughes, Jr., to venture into the aerospace and movie business. A famous Howard Hughes quote is, "We don't have a monopoly. Anyone who wants to dig a well without a Hughes bit can always use a pick and shovel."

It is known that Hughes suffered near-fatal injuries as the pilot of an experimental plane that crashed in 1946. The crash into two homes in Beverly Hills, California, left Hughes with serious pain and suffering for the remainder of his thirty years. The crash was dramatized in the 2004 biopic about Hughes, *The Aviator*, directed by Martin Scorsese, and starring Leonardo DiCaprio. Hughes later became a recluse and was said to have been heavily medicated with pain-relieving drugs until his death in 1976. It has been reported that after a major hip operation in 1973, he never walked again.

Hughes was known to be severely neurotic. He continued to control his empire as a recluse, with key personnel, many of

175

whom had worked for him from his early days. He was known to be loyal and generous in compensation, but gave no stock options to stock investors.

It has been alleged that Hughes suffered from a psychiatric disorder known as Obsessive Compulsive Disorder, or OCD. It manifests in obsessive thoughts and compulsive behavior.

Hughes was typical of many of the pioneering oil industry titans who gave part of their wealth for the betterment of humankind. In 1953, he created the Howard Hughes Medical Institute (HHMI). Its charter states:

> *The primary purpose and objective of the Howard Hughes Medical Institute shall be the promotion of human knowledge within the field of the basic sciences (principally the field of medical research and medical education) and the effective application thereof for the benefit of mankind.*

At the end of fiscal year 2015, the institute had $18.2 billion in diversified net assets, making it the nation's largest private supporter of academic biomedical research. In the past ten years, the institute has provided almost $8 billion in direct support for research and science education. HHMI is one of the largest philanthropies in the world.

Movies, books, and stories of Hughes abound with accounts of his eccentraries. One of my favorite stories is about alligators. Hughes born and raised in Houston, was familiar with Cajun stories of alligators. There is an old saying "When you're up to your neck in alligators, it's easy to forget that the initial objective was to drain the pond." Recently, it has been resurrected partially by Donald Trump in his talk of "draining the swamp." There is an alligator story out there about Hughes and girlfriend, actress Terry Moore, exchanging alligator mating calls. Terry would make the female's soft hoot and clicking sound. Hughes played the deep-voiced male, bellowing loudly.

Probably no name like the *Hughes Glomar Explorer* recalls more Cold War intrigue and adventure. The story is not over, as the CIA has not released all its data surrounding the incident. We may never know the full story, but our children might. The CIA has a sense of humor. Back in June 2014, the CIA's first tweet was a "we can neither confirm nor deny." The "neither confirm nor deny" language is a deflection journalists are used to receiving when they inquire about potentially classified information. The phrase has its roots in a CIA effort to cover up their efforts to retrieve a sunken Soviet submarine with the *Hughes Glomar Explorer.*

The CIA's David Sharp was on the ground floor of Project Azorian, the code name the agency bestowed upon its plan to recover *K-129*. He is the only CIA employee ever given a green light to write a book about it - *The CIA's Greatest Covert Operation: Inside the Daring Mission to Recover a Nuclear-Armed Soviet Sub*. According to Sharp:

"There are small but great moments in history when some few have dared to do the impossible. This book is a record of one of those moments. Project Azorian — the monumentally audacious six-year mission to recover the sub and learn its secrets—has been celebrated within the CIA as its greatest covert operation."

Interestingly, there were no engineered specifications given to Global Marine. Apparently, the CIA told Global Marine what they wanted and left the design and construction to them. One of the stories is that Global Marine planned for Levingston Shipbuilding Co. to build it, but the Hughes interests, namely the Summa Corporation, preferred Sun Shipbuilding Co., in Philadelphia, owned by the wealthy Pew family. The Sun company was founded in 1901 by pioneers in the new Spindletop Oilfield in Beaumont, Texas.

According to Sharp, he "using an alias identity, managed the eighty-five-man program office in Los Angeles that was responsible for directing the sea trials and integrated system testing of the ship (*Hughes Glomar Explorer*) and the claw that would be used to capture the sunken submarine."

Project Azorian, was so secret its existence was not declassified until February 2010, and much of the data is still top-secret. To this day, many of the files, photographs, videotapes, and other documentary evidence remain closed to the public. The costs have never been revealed. Estimates have ranged as high as an "unbelievable" $800 million, which in 2016 dollars would be $4.8 billion.

The USS *Halibut* steamed to the area and, upon locating the sunken submarine, took twenty thousand photos. Only a few photos have been released to the public. It is reported that something happened around the missile tubes.

The story began on March 11, 1968, when, with *K-129*, a Soviet Golf II-class submarine carrying three SS-N-4 nuclear-armed ballistic missiles with one megaton warheads, exploded and rapidly sank. The nuclear warheads had about eighty times the blast power of the atomic bomb dropped on Hiroshima in 1945. The U.S. Navy located the submarine about 1,500 miles northwest of Hawaii on the ocean floor, 16,500 feet below the surface. The *K-129* had sailed from the naval base at Petropavlovsk on Russia's Kamchatka Peninsula. For six years, *K-129* rested on the ocean bottom. No one had retrieved anything from that depth. What would the Russians do if they found out? But dreams of recovering the Russian sub within the U.S. military establishment floated around for years.

Conspiracy theories have swirled around Project Azorian, filling the void where official silence has reigned. One of them is promulgated in the 2005 book *Red Star Rogue*, by Kenneth Sewell and Clint Richmond. They posit that the *K-129* was taken over by rogue Stalinist KGB agents to start a nuclear conflict. But the conflict was to be between the United States and China, as, per the authors, the sub had the power to disguise its sonic signature as a Chinese Navy vessel. The story of the *K-129* being a rogue Russian submarine has been discredited by both Russian and American personnel. But the fact that the CIA has never released all the secret data gives room for conspiracy theorists to continue the theory.

In a BBC interview recorded in February 2013, Commander-in-Chief of the Soviet Navy at the time, Vladimir Chernavin, says the accident was caused by a malfunction in a missile tube and makes no mention of a collision with an American submarine.

The interview was conducted for the BBC2 series *The Silent War*. The recovery system was a large pipe extended down from the ship. At the end of the pipe was a mammoth claw known as the capture vehicle, or "Clementine". It was designed to scoop the Russian sub and cradle it on its journey up. It was reported that only the forward 40-foot section of the bow was recovered. It seems that at 5,000 feet, the *K-129* sub broke into several pieces when the claw contraption failed. A subcontractor in California had designed and built the claw. Also, the recovered section was radioactively contaminated with what turned out to be weapons-grade plutonium. This would certainly indicate that some sort of catastrophic event took place. The CIA history is silent on the cause of the accident.

In October 1992, Robert Gates, CIA director, visited Moscow to meet with President Boris Yeltsin of Russia. He gave him the photographs of the bodies of the Russians. In his 1996 book, *From the Shadows,* Robert Gates says:

> As a gesture of intent, a symbol of a new era, I carried with me the Soviet naval flag that had shrouded the coffins of the half dozen Soviet sailors whose remains the Glomar Explorer had recovered when it raised part of a Soviet ballistic missile submarine from deep in the Pacific Ocean in the mid-1970's. I also was taking to Yeltsin a videotape of their burial at sea, complete with prayers for the dead and the Soviet national anthem—a dignified and respectful service even at the height of the Cold War."

The prototype for the *Hughes Glomar Explorer* was the state-of-the-art *Glomar Challenger.* Levingston was in the process of building eight drillships for Global Marine, of which *Glomar*

Challenger was the third. Near the center of the *Explorer* was the moon pool, a large 23-foot opening in the bottom of the ship. The moon pool was enlarged to lift the submerged submarine.

A mystery is how they located the precise location of the Russian sub. Jim Davis, a leading patent attorney represented Roger Bascom in a patent lawsuit claiming patent violation. The issue was whether the *Hughes Glomar Explorer* located the Russian sub in 16,000 feet of water. CIA alleged that an espionage Hunter-Killer sub with a state-of the art sonar with under water nuclear weapons found the sub. The logs of the vessels were not allowed for both the drill ship and the sub and the case was dismissed. Roger Bascom was one of the originators of the Mohole drill program and wrote a book in January 1961, *A Hole in the Bottom of the Sea: The Story of the Mohole Project.*

One of the stories is that David Packard got excited about the *Glomar Challenger* and the *Hughes Glomar Explorer* adventures. Packard was co-founder in 1939 of Hewlett-Packard (HP), which became a leader in technology and corporate culture, inspiring innovators, and entrepreneurs around the globe. The 9100A is now recognized throughout the industry as the first desktop computer. In December 2000, *Wired Magazine* named it the first personal computer.

Packard's interest in deep-sea technology began after Melvin Laird, the Secretary of Defense, asked him to come to Washington in 1969 to serve as his deputy. While at the Pentagon he had oversight of the *Glomar Explorer's* secret recovery of part of a sunken Soviet submarine. Packard by necessity became familiar with the prospects and limitations of deep-sea work. He was proud of that operation and enjoyed telling guardedly cryptic stories about it later. ("How One Man Made a Difference: David Packard," Marcia McNutt, Monterey Bay Aquarium Research Institution, Moss Landing, California. Presented at the symposium "Oceanography: The Making of a Science" February 8, 2000, Scripps Institution of Oceanography, La Jolla, California.)

Later, Packard became personally involved in ocean research, founding the Monterey Bay Aquarium Research Institute (MBARI) and bringing onto the board of directors Walter H. Munk, from the Scripps Institution of Oceanography, who is credited with starting the Mohole Project resulting in the *Glomar Challenger* scientific drillship and its step-sister the *Glomar Explorer*. Today, the David and Lucille Packard Foundation contributes grants to MBARI averaging around $40 million per year. Packard was quoted as saying that MBARI was set up to explore the biology, chemistry, and physics of Monterey Bay and the contiguous waters beyond. David referred to the "mystery" and "frontiers" of the deep ocean and processes which "await discovery." (http://www.tos.org/oceanography/archive/2-2_munk2.pdf).

An old friend of mine, Larry Kelley, was helpful in this book. Kelley's father was an independent oil operator, buying oil leases and drilling wells. He had one big client, the personal account of Howard Hughes, with whom Kelley dealt directly. Global Marine was founded in Los Angeles before moving to Houston, and Hughes and Global Marine had business relations.

As a young man working for Global Marine, Kelley would go around to different oil companies and make presentations soliciting work for the Glomar drill ships. He had a projector and film about the *Glomar Challenger*. Kelley tells how the oilmen were fascinated by its ability to hold a steady position with the dynamic positioning system. It must be completely reliable to be effective, in even the most extreme weather conditions. However, he remembers that only one man, who worked for Humble, was curious enough to ask about the dynamic position computer. Kelley says he was obviously very knowledgeable about computers and was very impressed with the presentation about the *Glomar Challenger*. In fact, Kelley made a deal to lease the *Glomar Grand Banks* to drill for Humble. Few engineers at that time were familiar with the software capabilities of computers. Of course, there were no plans for ultra-deep drilling that would require that capability. In shallow waters, where most of the offshore drilling was done, anchors were used. Kelley was one of many former Global Marine employees who went on to a leadership position in the oil and gas business. Kelley started up an onshore drilling company, and is still personally active in oil and gas production.

Another employee of Global Marine who went on to an illustrious career in the offshore oil business was John Horton Atwood, who played football and baseball at Purdue University. John was a Pi Tau Sigma Scholastic Mechanical Engineering student at Purdue, where he graduated with honors in 1951 with a BSME degree. In 2007, Purdue recognized John as one of its outstanding mechanical engineers. John played two seasons of professional football for the NFL's New York Giants. He was an executive vice president with Global Marine, and founded Atwood Oceanic in 1968.

Thomas P. Richards, after graduating from Texas A&M University in 1966 with a degree in marketing, started his oil career as a roughneck with Global SantaFe (then Global Marine) in January 1966. He worked for a couple of years, and then was involved in the construction of three of the company's drillships in Orange, Texas, including the *Glomar Challenger*. Richards was the one who brought to my attention that the *Glomar Challenger* was the granddaddy of today's drillships. Richards can name many of the individuals he worked with at Levingston Shipbuilding and Global Marine during those days. He fondly remembers those times as the early careers of young men having lots of fun and doing innovative and creative things. At the time, they were building rigs with no standards or complete specifications. They were setting the standards and the specifications. It demanded the best of known technology and work to do things that had never been done before.

Richards led the drilling company Grey Wolf as chairman, president, and chief executive, selling the company for $2 billion in cash and stock in 1998 to Precision Drilling Trust, headquartered in Calgary, Alberta, at the time. Richards has been named Contractor of the Year by IADC—the International Association of Drilling Contractors. Established in 1988, this annual award is sponsored by Schlumberger Oilfield Services and IADC to recognize individual drilling contractors' outstanding lifetime achievements in technical innovation, safety, and economic efficiency within the drilling industry. It is the only prestigious industry award reserved exclusively for drilling contractors.

The data from the *JOIDES Resolution's* ocean drilling continues the mission of offering a scientific means of understanding climate and environmental change throughout a significant part of our planet's history—a research subject often termed Earth's paleoclimate. The *JR's* core samples are the "smoking gun" in evaluating many historical events related to paleoclimate, changes in the solid earth and more, such as the extinction of the dinosaurs and plate tectonics. Like its namesake, the purpose of the current *JOIDES Resolution* is to sail for scientific exploration. This time, those discoveries lie beneath the ocean floor.

The *JR* began working for the Ocean Drilling Program (ODP) in 1985. Drilling with ODP continued until September 2003, at which point the Integrated Ocean Drilling Program (IODP) began. IODP is an international research program that explores the history and structure of the earth as recorded in seafloor sediments and rocks.

JOIDES Resolution's complement can consist of fifty scientists and technicians and sixty-five crew members. The crew consists of marine professionals and ocean drilling specialists, among others. The *JR's* science party is specific to each mission, with skills and science disciplines chosen especially to best achieve the mission's goals. The *JR* has a large array of tools through a subcontract with Schlumberger LWD (abbreviation for logging while drilling) operations. Schlumberger LWD provides real time data from geological logs and other downhole measurements on both the *JR* and the *Chikyu*.

For the second ship, the Japanese stepped up to the plate and designed and built a brand new scientific drillship at an estimated cost of $500 million. It was named the *Chikyu* and began operations in 2005. A scale model of the *Chikyu* is on exhibit in the Sant Ocean Hall in the Smithsonian Institution's National Museum of Natural History, Washington, DC, which opened in September 2008. As requested by the Japan Federation of Economic Organizations, the authorized corporation, the Japan Marine Science and Technology Center, (JAMESTEC) was established based on the government and industrial investments and contributions and operates the *Chikyu*.

Acting as the principal vessel of the International Ocean Discovery Program (IODP), the main objective of the *Chikyu* is to facilitate a wide range of activities that will contribute to the future of humankind. These activities may include revealing the mechanism that causes giant earthquakes, the origins of life, future global environmental changes, and new deep sea resources. IODP builds upon the legacies of *Glomar Challenger* drilling voyages. The Science Plan for the International Ocean Discovery Program, *Illuminating Earth's Past, Present, and Future*, is intended to guide international collaboration on scientific ocean drilling during the period 2013-2023. It was crafted on behalf of earth, ocean, atmospheric, and life scientists at the request of science funding agencies from twenty four nations.

24

Cecil H. Green

Imagine living in 1958, and knowing that the integrated circuit--the microchip--was about to be invented, and would revolutionize the world. Newly employed by Texas Instruments, Jack St. Clair Kilby recorded his initial ideas concerning the integrated circuit in July of that year. Kilby's idea was to make all components and the chip out of the same block of semiconductor material. A year later, another engineer, Robert Noyce, came up with an idea that improved Kilby's circuit. And so, the digital revolution was born. Noyce later co-founded Intel with the famous Gordon E. Moore, who gave us the well-known quote "Moore's law," predicting that the capacity of chips would double every two years and the price would stay almost the same. In 2016, the sixth-generation Intel chip offered 3,500 times more performance than a chip in 1971. Microchips (microprocessors) have led the exponential growth rate of the power of computers' programs and memory. Digital information with the recording, storage, and dissemination of information has become practically free.

Cecil Green brought the confidence and experience of someone who was in on the pioneering of the computer industry. Green, co-founder of Texas Instruments, had retired to LaJolla, California. Green became one of Walter Munk's best friends, and a major benefactor of the Scripps Institution of Oceanography. Green had a deep interest and experience in ocean research. He had worked in oil offshore seismic work as a partner of GSI, a geophysical company in the thirties, before forming TI in 1941. Green was a financial benefactor of tens of millions of dollars for the Scripps Institution of Oceanography. He retired to La Jolla and died there in 2003 at the age of 102.

The Cecil H. and Ida M. Green Foundation for Earth Sciences supports visiting scholars and resident scientists at the La Jolla branch of the University of California's multi-campus Institute of Geophysics and Planetary Physics (IGPP).

Cecil Green was a supporter of the creation of the Mohole Project that evolved into the Deep-Water Drilling Project with the *Glomar Challenger* drillship. Green had Texas Instruments make one of the proposals to co-manage the second phase of the Mohole project. He was famous for his ability to enlist the help of other people. Evidence of his cheerleading of oceanography and deepwater drilling can be found in numerous buildings he supported and contributed to financially. Green funded the Cecil H. and Ida M. Green Institute of Geophysics and Planetary Physics (IGPP). The Scripps institution of Oceanography branch of IGPP was dedicated in 1964. It was headed by their good friend, Walter Munk. This foundation still supports the IGPP with a $10 million foundation. Green lived his last years at his residence and he died in a hospital he endowed, the Scripps Green Hospital in La Jolla, California.

He helped found the University of Texas at Dallas, Green College at the University of British Columbia, St. Mark's School of Texas, and Green College at the University of Oxford. The Greens were also major contributors to the Cecil H. Green Library at Stanford University.

MIT - Cecil and Ida Green Center for Earth Sciences

At MIT, the Greens provided major funding for the 295-foot-tall Cecil H. and Ida F. Green Center for Earth Sciences, designed by I.M. Pei. The Earth Sciences building opened in 1962. Green requested that "it must look like an earth science building." The building is the highest in Cambridge, Massachusetts.

In 1973, Texas A&M University completed their fifteen-story oceanography building in College Station, costing $8.5 million. In the mid-1960's, Texas A&M president, General James Earl Rudder, had talked with "Doc" Ewing about coming to Texas A&M and putting in an ocean research facility like the one Ewing founded and headed at Lamont-Doherty at Columbia University. Since its founding in 1949, Lamont-Doherty has been a leader in the earth sciences. During Ewing's twenty-five years as the founding director, Lamont-Doherty oceanographers developed techniques for seagoing studies, built equipment for continuous echo sounding, precision depth recording, seismic reflection and refraction measurements, ocean bottom seismographs, piston coring of seafloor sediment, and gravity and magnetic measurements of the ocean floor. Perhaps more than any other individual, Ewing laid the foundation for the revolutionary concept known as plate tectonics.

The deal at A&M fell through, but a few years later Ewing retired from Lamont-Doherty, and made an agreement with the University of Texas in 1972 to run the newly formed UT-Divisions of Earth and Planetary Sciences in Galveston. A four-story structure was built and named Ewing Hall, at 301 University Boulevard, Galveston, Texas. It is now part of the University of Texas Medical Branch (UTMB).

For years, people spoke of an old sea captain—some say maybe even gentleman pirate, Jean Lafitte, himself, who willed his land to his children and asked them to keep it in the family. But eventually one of his heirs sold the land, against the captain's wishes, making his spirit angry. This was the land Ewing Hall was built on. Supposedly, his ghost appears on the wall of the building. Ewing was born in Lockney, Texas, and graduated from Rice University in Houston. He died in 1974 in Galveston, Texas.

Texas A&M established a marine research center in Galveston cofounded by Dr. Sammy Ray, a world-renowned marine biologist specializing in oysters. When the oil industry was hit with a series of lawsuits placing the blame of oyster mortality on oil companies, Texas A&M found that a parasite -dermocystidium marium - infested oyster beds and was responsible. This won the favor of oil companies and the need for ocean research.

Support for the Texas A&M Oceanography Department received the necessary funding from industry and the federal government. Offshore oil drilling was concerned with weather – wave strength and size - and pushed for hurricane studies. Hurricanes have produced waves in the Gulf of Mexico reaching 100 feet in height.

Cecil Green helped fund Ewing Hall. The Greens also funded the *Ida Green* Research vessel for research from the Galveston location. *Ida Green* is a 135-foot research vessel that operates out of the Galveston Geophysics Laboratory, a Division of Earth and Planetary Sciences of the Marine Biomedical Institute (Marine Science Institute), University of Texas.

Educated as an electrical engineer, Green became known for geosciences. He first got involved in ocean research in 1930 when he cofounded Geophysical Service to pioneer reflection seismology for the oil industry off the coast of California. *Seismic* is defined as pertaining to, of the nature of, or caused by an earthquake or vibration of the earth, whether due to natural or artificial causes.

It has been said that Cecil Green was the one who first found oil in Arabia. He never said that. The facts are that the Standard Oil Company of California (SOCAL) contracted with Cecil's company, GSI (Geophysical Services, Inc.), for a geophysical survey in Arabia.

Sadad Husseini, Aramco executive vice president of Exploration and Production and an Aramco director, said in the March 30, 1988, edition of Aramco's publication, *The Arabian Sun*, "Cecil Green is truly one of the pioneers of exploration." Husseini was a geologist talking to geophysicists. The members of the two schools of thought were frequently at odds with each other. Green was quoted as saying that back in the 1930's, geologists didn't have much respect for geophysicists. "They thought geophysics was a lot of black magic box."

The first oil well in Saudi Arabia was the Dammam No. 7, where the SOCAL drillers finally struck oil on March 3, 1938. Cecil Green and his company, GSI, were there on the ground at the beginning. Green traveled to Saudi Arabia in 1930 with an oil exploration crew for Geophysical Services in Dallas, a pioneer in digital analysis of seismic records. SOCAL was using GSI for their seismic work.

Following World War II, GSI acquired a license to build transistors that ultimately resulted in the birth of Texas Instruments, of which GSI then became a subsidiary. TI sold GSI, and it is now a part of Schlumberger.

Texas Instruments' Jack St. Clair Kilby, invented integrated circuits in 1958. TI introduced the first transistor radios in 1954 and the portable, hand-held electronic calculator in

1967. TI and, later, Intel, founded in 1968, led the world's pioneering of the commercial silicon transistor. The market capitalization (2015) for Texas instruments was around $55 billion and of Intel, about $150 billion.

In 1968, the Society of Exploration Geophysicists, which has around 33,000 members, awarded to Cecil Green the first Maurice Ewing Medal, which had been recently created as a major medal of the SEG "to be awarded from time to time to a person who is deserving of special recognition through having made major contributions to the advancement of science and the profession of Exploration Geophysics." The citation accompanying the presentation of the Ewing Medal to Cecil Green concludes, "He has done more to advance the profession of exploration geophysics than any other living person."

The American Geophysical Union (AGU) also awards a prestigious Maurice Ewing Medal. This medal is given annually to recognize "significant original contributions to the ocean sciences," including "the advancement of oceanographic engineering, technology, and instrumentation, as well as outstanding service to the marine sciences." Walter Munk was the first recipient of this medal in 1974, the year that Maurice Ewing died. ("Maurice Ewing Medal" in *Awards Citations of SEG* (1998) SEG Press, Tulsa, OK.)

Robert R. Shrock, author of the book *Philanthropists Extraordinary*, a biography of Cecil and Ida Green, talks about their dozens of contributions to their fellow man. A list of the value they had contributed in 1985 totaled well over $150 million.

25
Levingston Goes to Singapore

Singapore's history reaches far back before its independence in 1965. This former colony was founded as a trading outpost of the British Empire nearly 200 years ago. In 1963 it became a state in the Federation of Malaysia but was expelled in 1965 and formed its own republic.

In World War II, an historical military event took place. Winston Churchill called the ignominious fall of Singapore to the Japanese the "worst disaster" and "largest capitulation" in British military history. Singapore had been touted by the British as their stronghold and nicknamed the "Gibraltar of the East." Few Americans know that the Japanese undertook one of their most ambitious military operations in December of 1941, carrying out almost simultaneous attacks with the bombing of Pearl Harbor on Sunday, the 7th, over ten thousand miles away. The fighting in Singapore lasted from December to February 9, 1942, although this was preceded by two months of British resistance as Japanese forces advanced down the Malay Peninsula. On February 15, 1942, the largest surrender of British-led forces in history took place. About eighty thousand British, Indian, and Australian troops became prisoners of war, joining fifty thousand taken by the Japanese in the earlier Malayan Campaign. The myth of the invincibility of the European soldier was shattered, and over eighty thousand British and Commonwealth troops were to spend the rest of the war in captivity. Half of them would never return home. Some critics have said there seems to be no doubt that, by sacrificing Singapore, Churchill single-handedly and unwittingly rang the final death knell of the British Empire whose power he strove to perpetuate.

The island endured three and half years of brutal Japanese occupation which included a massacre of its Chinese population, a massacre that was to claim up to seventy thousand lives. The island was to remain under occupation until soon after Japan's surrender to the Americans in August, 1945. The United States returned the island to the British. The decades after the war saw a political awakening among the local populace, and the rise of anti-colonial and nationalist sentiments.

Where is Singapore? Singapore is an island nation, both a city and a country, located just off the southern tip of Malaysia in Southeast Asia. The straight-line distance from Orange, Texas, to Singapore is ten thousand miles, crossing time zones with a thirteen-hour time difference: 1:00 pm in Orange is 2:00 am in Singapore of the next morning.

At the beginning of Singapore as a nation city, in 1965, the petroleum industry was almost nonexistent. Singapore back then has been described as little more than an impoverished swampy island with two million inhabitants and virtually

195

no natural resources. It became an independent island city-state in 1965, after being kicked out of the Malaysia government only three years after joining. Prior to that, it had been a British colony until 1962. At that time, Britain decided to close its military bases in Singapore within three years. It was estimated that the British military accounted for 20 percent of the Singaporean economy.

Upon their independence from Malaysia, Singapore faced a small domestic market, and high levels of unemployment and poverty. Seventy percent of Singapore's households lived in badly overcrowded conditions, and a third of its people squatted in slums on the city fringes. Unemployment averaged 14 percent, GDP per capita was US $516, and half of the population was illiterate. ("Economy of Singapore" from Wikipedia, the free encyclopedia)

The power of the communists was rapidly growing in Singapore. There were race riots between Malaysian and Chinese youths in 1969. In total, the violence killed thirty-six people and injured another 556.

In this environment, Lee Kuan Yew, educated in Britain, was first elected prime minister in 1963, and re-elected repeatedly until his retirement in 2000. Today, in 2016 the cultural mix is Chinese 76%, Malay 15%, Indian 6%, and other, 3%. The English of Singapore, SingEng or Singlish, is the common language of the multiethnic population and one of the four official languages that also includes Malay, Mandarin Chinese, and Tamil.

Word has gotten out that gum chewing is finable in Singapore. While that is not true, you can get fined $500 if you drop gum on the ground or stick it under a chair or table. Singapore is famous for being fastidious when it comes to urban cleanliness.

Rupert Murdoch, Chairman and Chief Executive Officer of News Corporation says:

"Lee Kuan Yew transformed what was a poor, decrepit colony (of Great Britain) into a shining, rich, and modern metropolis—at the time surrounded by hostile powers. With his brilliant, incisive intellect, he is one of the world's most outspoken and respected statesmen. This book is a 'must read' for any student of modern Asia." An endorsement of Lee's *From Third World to First: The Singapore Story: 1965–2000, 2000)*

By the end of the 1960's, Levingston Shipbuilding Company had reached the pinnacle of shipbuilding success. The offshore oil boom, along with the construction of several deep-sea research vessels, had provided the company with a backlog of construction contracts and years of consistent work and growth. At times, the management took a back seat, as the superintendents effectively ran the shipyard and delivered major projects repeatedly. With a workforce of more than two thousand, many of whom were Cajuns from southwest Louisiana, Levingston seemingly cranked out drilling rigs, offshore service vessels, and barges on a regular basis.

Meanwhile, some within the company began looking beyond the Gulf of Mexico for the next boom market and the next batch of construction work. Larry Baker, a Nebraska native who started at Levingston after World War II as a laborer making eighty cents an hour, had worked his way up the chain to become a top salesman. His wife, Virginia, also moved up the ranks in the company to become a senior accountant. Baker traveled everywhere searching for new markets and new customers. "You can make more money selling your expertise than you ever can doing it yourself," Baker said during a 2015 interview. "What we needed to do was to sell the knowledge that we had." In the late 1960's, he met an enthusiastic businessman from Singapore named K. C. Lee who had a connection to the developing shipbuilding industry in Asia. The two ultimately developed a business relationship that led Levingston—and the Bakers—to the Far East.

Lee's shipbuilding firm had limited capacity to manage and deliver projects on time and within budget. It needed some outside expertise to complete the projects and to show a pathway to growth. Baker and Lee agreed to have some of Levingston's skilled people transfer to Singapore under a management contract to help the yard get through its problems and develop new business. "We would furnish you people," Baker explained, referring to the management agreement. "If you needed an electrician, we would send you a Cajun electrician who's been doing this. He is not a certified fourteen--carat gold engineer electrician; he knows how to put electrical in the rig. He doesn't know how to put it on paper, he just knows how to do that. That's what they needed…not somebody who could write about it; they needed somebody who could do that."

Baker finalized the deal, and Ed Malloy, Chairman of the Board of Levingston, and Walter Pennington, President, gave the okay in 1968. The parties agreed to enter a joint venture that was called Far East Levingston Shipbuilding. The use of the Levingston name gave the venture immense credibility. Baker put together the management team under David Crawford, hired the craftsmen from the yard and structured the actual contract. At the last moment, however, his counterpart threw him a curve ball. "When we sat down to do the deal and sign," Baker recalled, "K. C. Lee said, 'No, it is a deal only if you come, Larry Baker." Baker was taken aback. He talked the idea over with his wife, who agreed to move to Singapore for three years to do the job. "I made the deal because it was good for Levingston," Baker emphatically said. "I had been there for over twenty-five years, and my heart and soul were in Levingston, just like everybody else down there. And I wanted Levingston to do well, so I made a deal that was good for them."

Baker brought seventeen workers with skills such as welding, layout, piping, electrical, painting, inventory control, and engineering over to Singapore to teach Singaporeans the needed abilities for working in the shipyard. The yard consisted of a twenty-four-acre site located in the Jurong industrial district and employed roughly nine hundred workers, performing various construction jobs such as building barges and oil rigs.

When they got to Singapore, Lee had hired many young engineering graduates to work with the craftsmen from Orange. Literacy of English enabled the Singaporeans to quickly pick up the names of the work and product identification. Particularly difficult for them were the nicknames involving the slang of the oil field. But their English language proficiency allowed the Singaporeans to absorb information at a phenomenal rate.

The group from Texas quickly sensed that the island nation was in a transition and struggling with economic stagnation. Singapore, a newly formed country, was losing jobs. The British were closing their military facilities, which accounted for 20 percent of Singapore's gross national product. The per capita income of the country at that time was around $2,500 per person, with a population of around two million people.

The entry of Levingston into Singapore happened at a critical time in that island nation's history. The country had been an independent republic for only a few years. The People's Action Party controlled the state and still does to this day. The one-party state has, however, provided the people with tremendous prosperity through forward-thinking social and economic development policies that worked. Levingston played a major role in Singapore's transformation into an industrial society, with shipbuilding as a major economic engine.

K.C. Lee, the president of Far East Levingston Shipbuilding Company, had raised money from wealthy Chinese investors paying high interest rates. Lee raised equity from a public offering on the Singapore Exchange. For the use of Levingston's brand and Levingston personnel running the company, Levingston received a percent of sales. Far East Levingston as a company had expanded rapidly, requiring massive investments in assets. K.C. Lee needed working capital, and demanded that Levingston buy 40 percent of the equity. After much discussion, the board of Levingston back in Texas decided not to make the investment. K. C. Lee did not renew the Levingston management contract. To financially survive, Far East Levingston Shipbuilding (Fels) sold 40 percent of their equity to the Keppel Corporation in 1972. In 1996 they changed the name to Keppel (FELS). In 2001, Keppel (FELS) was privatized by Keppel Corporation and became its wholly owned subsidiary.

"The vision then was to develop Singapore as a base for the offshore industry comparable to Houston, which is often regarded as the center for the oil exploration industry. Keppel's aim at that time was to provide experienced personnel, facilities, and services to offshore drilling contractors and oil company services of a quality and at a standard of efficiency that the industry was accustomed to in the US." (Speech by Mr. Lim Chee Onn, Executive Chairman of Keppel Corporation at the launch of the Keppel Professorship and the Keppel FELS Book at Keppel FELS Pioneer Yard on September 19, 2002.)

In 2017, Keppel FELS is a subsidiary of Keppel Offshore & Marine Ltd. (Keppel O&M), a wholly owned company of Keppel Corporation Limited. Singapore's Keppel FELS is officially the world's largest manufacturer of offshore rigs by rig delivery count, per Guinness' World Records, for delivering twenty-one offshore rigs to its customers in 2013.

Lee Kuan Yew was a real visionary and the first prime minister of Singapore. In promoting his economic development plan to the United States, he said, "I don't want your money; I want your jobs. I want to put my people to work. Send us jobs, send us work. That's what we want to do. We want to work," Baker, Jr. recounted that Yew instilled in the people a good work ethic, and the government provided subsidies only for those families who desperately needed help. All others worked. His policies endured, building a successful industrial economy in a few decades. In 2012, the nation's average income per capita grew to $56,694 dollars a year with a population of 3.8 million Singaporeans and 1.5 million foreigners. This compares to an average U.S. income per capita of $46,860 dollars a year.

George Yao, prominent Singapore politician, told a conference of the Lee Kuan Yew School of Public Policy in October 2014, "Ultimately, what drives Singapore, what gives Singapore our special advantage, is the ability to arbitrage across cultures." Yao is a Catholic and was recently named by Pope Francis to serve on the Lay Members Board of the newly established Council for Economic Affairs.

When the bottom fell out of the oil market in the early 1980's, the Singapore shipyard struggled to stay afloat. A young executive named Choo Chiau Beng, with degrees from the University of Newcastle and Harvard Business School, convinced the board of FELS (now Keppel Corporation) not to sell off the shipyard, but to keep it going. He argued that they should keep the team together and build drilling rigs for inventory. The gamble paid off. Keppel later became one of the top companies for building offshore drilling rigs around the world. In 1992, the company established a shipyard in Brownsville, Texas. The Singapore government took complete control of the company in 1997, renaming Far East Levingston Shipbuilding Company as Keppel FELS, Ltd., using the name of the holding company—Keppel—with the initials of Far East Levingston Shipbuilding.

This new business venture overseas had implications for Levingston. It broadened the exposure of the company's homegrown expertise in shipbuilding and offshore marine construction to a growing global market. Three decades later, the remnants of Levingston's excellence in engineering and mastery of shipbuilding can still be felt around the world in the international offshore oil and gas industry. The Singapore project also gave Larry Baker, Sr. the opportunity to expand beyond Levingston and create his own offshore rig construction company, Baker Marine Corporation. Baker went on to pioneer a revolutionary drilling rig, the Baker three-legged jack-up drilling rig. Many of the original sixty-two jack-ups built at the Baker Marine shipyard in Ingleside, Texas, are still in operation today. Other products were developed, such as the Baker Marine offshore crane, anchor winch, direct drive crane winches, and horizontal drilling units.

Larry Baker, Sr. and the Levingston crew worked at the Singapore yard for three years and completed several vessels and drilling rigs. During that time, however, the Orange shipyard had changed management and was losing money. Ed Malloy had essentially left the company. He died in early 1973. There ensued an internal power struggle for control of Levingston among the top executives, including Baker. "Levingston had lost plenty," Baker recalled, "and we [Far East Levingston] had made millions over there. Bobby Jones wanted to be chairman of the board, and he got enough stroke to where he could fire George Brown, Chairman of the Board, and Malcolm Vaughan, President, and me, and Virginia Baker, all of us."

Baker regrouped and through his many connections met with I.H.C. Holland, which had a shipyard at Ingleside Point near Corpus Christi, Texas, to discuss a management position. The company was building the first of three large three-hundred-foot jack-up rigs. Midway through the first project for Penrod Drilling, the shipyard ran into significant cost overruns. Baker was hired as general manager to take over and finish the project and complete the additional jack-ups: one for Petrobras (the Brazilian National Oil Company) and one for Maersk Drilling. Shortly thereafter, he negotiated to purchase the shipyard from the Dutch company, started Baker Marine Corporation, and began designing and building specialized jack-up rigs of his own. He brought in several former Levingston people, including Malcolm Vaughan and Bob Fogal, to help him start the company.

Baker Marine started as a small operation, but by the late 1970's, it was one of the leading dealers and fabricators in jack-up rigs in the world. Larry Baker, Jr., attributed the company's success to the quality of the I.H.C. Holland/Le Tourneau product, which his father purchased with the yard. He said, "It was a hell of a product that we got, in that these little darlings were revolutionary. They weren't the only ones, but they were hell on wheels."

During the 1970's, Baker Marine became so busy that it did not have the time nor the space to fill all its orders, and had to contract other companies to complete different parts of its jobs. Baker, Jr. remembered that, for one marine drilling project, Levingston built the mat, Baker Marine constructed the platform, a French company made the legs, and then they brought all the parts to the Ingleside yard for final assembly.

Over time, Baker Marine began building pieces in Singapore and at its other international yards, including South Africa, Egypt, China, and Brazil, because foreign governments offered incentives and cheap labor that lowered costs and increased earnings significantly.

In 1982, with the coming oil price crunch and the historic downturn in drilling, Larry Baker sold his company. Most of Baker's jack-ups ended up in the Gulf of Mexico, some went to Africa, others landed in the Persian Gulf, and a few drilled off the coast of Indonesia. During its heyday, the company was building a quarter of the jack-up drilling rigs for the global offshore oil and gas industry.

Baker, Sr., who in March 2015, celebrated his ninetieth birthday, recounted the experience of pioneering offshore drilling rigs at Levingston and at Baker Marine. "We learned, we learned, we learned," Baker stated in an interview. In 1990, Baker and his wife, Virginia, retired to Vermillion Parish, south of Lafayette, Louisiana. They bought ten acres along Vermillion Bayou and named the residence Shangri-La after the five-star Shangri-La Hotel in Singapore.

Baker is one of the bigger-than-life characters who created the offshore oil drilling industry as we know it today. He was extremely disciplined. Baker would drink whiskeys with the oil boys, except his alcohol was actually colored water. Baker usually had a cigar in his hand but never smoked it. He stuck to "no womanizing, no drugs, no alcohol, no tobacco, no gambling" in a culture with strong peer pressure to partake. These vices ruined many brilliant lives.

One of the "drivers of success" that Baker learned during his years at Levingston was to "get common people to do uncommon things." That certainly was a characteristic of the Levingston people through the years. In the shipyard, most of the craftsmen were Cajuns from the swampy land of South Louisiana and farm boys from East Texas. They were smart, but had little or no formal education. It was the leaders and the "can-do" spirit at Levingston that drove these individuals to do uncommon things. Baker was also known to talk about three critical elements necessary for running a shipyard: chalk, money, and marbles. You needed chalk and a chalkboard to draw out your plans and designs for equipment that had never been built before. You needed money to keep the business growing. And you needed marbles, or "smarts," to make the right decisions at the right time. Levingston had all three.

26

Roy Huffington

Roy Huffington was a legendary Texas wildcatter. Born in Tomball, Texas, in 1917, he was a ringer for John Wayne, a hard drinker, a loud man, a large man, who worked all the time. Huffington started his oil career as a geologist for Humble Oil and Refining Company, now ExxonMobil. He did a lot of pioneering geological work in the Gulf of Mexico, through which he came to know the people at Levingston Shipbuilding. The Huffington tale is a classic in the lore of the oil wildcatter.

In an interview with *Forbes*, Huffington said he liked drilling for oil because of his fascination with geology: "It's good to peel back the earth and see the history of the world," he said, adding that by comparison, "our lifetimes are but a fraction of a second." He was not the typical Texas wildcatter in a big Stetson, shiny belt buckle, and cowboy boots. Huffington never wore boots or a Stetson; he was generous and caring and loved plants and animals.

In 1968, he approached Larry Baker, Sr., who had just started up Far East Levingston Shipbuilding in Singapore.

Huffington needed a tugboat and two fuel barges to supply fuel for the helicopters needed for furnishing his drilling rig with men and inventory. Huffington had signed a production-sharing contract with the Republic of Indonesia for 2,436 square miles of land. Shell Oil Company had produced oil from 8,500 feet for decades on the Indonesian lease and depleted the reserves. Huffington's theory was that there were oil and natural gas in deeper sand at 12,500 feet. Huffington felt the geological structure was like the Texas/Louisiana Gulf Coast, and if you went deeper, you would hit pay dirt. Huffington signed a production-sharing contract, which was rarely used in the oil business, with PERTAMINA, the Indonenesian State Oil Company. The Production Sharing Contract (PSC) shifts power away from the oil companies to the oil-producing states.

In his interview with, *Forbes* in 1977, Huffington said: "If the major oil companies didn't like what you wanted to do, they just didn't put up the money and that, they thought, would stop you." Huffington's production-sharing contract turned out to be a cause of an important shift in contracts for oil and gas drilling and production. Today, some form of production-sharing contract is the norm.

Huffington was successful in negotiating a thirty-year, production-sharing contract with PERTAMINA. The cost of the tugboat and barges was almost $1 million. Huffington informed Baker he did not have the money. Baker recalls having said, "Levingston doesn't need to practice building tugs and barges." Huffington explained the "wildcat" deal. All his resources would be tied up paying for drilling in palm swamps near the coast in East Kalimantan. But he needed fuel for the helicopters and the rig. The only way of getting the fuel was by water. Huffington wanted Larry Baker to help him raise money.

The drilling site was an isolated stretch of swamp and jungle. Baker told Huffington he would try to raise the money for the tugboat and barges. He went to the Singaporean partners and to Levingston to finance the tugboat and barges. They both refused. But George Brown, Jr., a Beaumont attorney for Levingston, told Baker he would personally put up a big chunk of the cost. Baker borrowed the other half from a bank, and they made a deal.

They set up the ownership of the equipment in Panama. They charged Huffington rental of $1 million a year for three years. The first year, Baker and Brown would get all their money back. At the end of three years, Huffington told Baker that he knew that they had taken advantage of him with excessive charges. Huffington felt that after the $3 million he paid, they should give him the tugboat and three barges. Baker and Brown agreed. Then Huffington told them that since no liens had been filed on the equipment, he had borrowed $1 million on them to help pay for the rig to drill the wildcat well. It had hit pay dirt with a huge natural gas reserve at Badak Field, East Kalimantan.

The first wildcat well was spudded November 27, 1971. It was drilled to 11,0210 feet deep and completed February 11, 1972. Huffington had originally sealed the deal with only $50,000 and a promise to invest millions to drill the wildcat wells. Huffington did not have the money and had to scramble, selling interests in the project and liquidating assets he owned. No oil company would invest in the arrangement because it was a shared-production deal and oil companies would only do purchases of mineral rights at that time. No doubt the agreement with Baker and Brown for the tugs and barges was critical for Huffington.

At an early stage, Huffington brought in Mobil Oil Company to help develop a liquid natural gas (LNG) project to export natural gas. Five years later, the first LNG shipment was sent to Japan. This started one of the first and most successful LNG plants in the world. From this venture, Indonesia became the largest exporter of LNG in the world, and Japan became the largest importer. For those unfamiliar with the term LNG, it is natural gas that has been temporarily converted into a liquid. This is done to save space: 610 cubic feet of natural gas can be converted into a single cubic foot of LNG. Converting natural gas into LNG makes it easier to store and easier to transport where pipelines are not available.

Larry Baker and George Brown did not suspect the helping hand they were providing would change the energy future of Asia when they gave the go-ahead to build and lease a tugboat and fuel barges for Roy Huffington. Huffington said he was lucky to be at the right place at the right time. Later, Huffington sold his interest in the project for around $600 million. The sale left him with a family fortune estimated at $500 million in 1989. At the time of the sale, Huffington claimed they had discovered about fifteen trillion cubic feet of natural gas and about five hundred million barrels of oil.

Roy Huffington died in 2008. His son, Michael, was married to Arianna Huffington, who started the *Huffington Post* on May 9, 2005, as a liberal/left commentary outlet. On February 7, 2011, AOL acquired the mass-market *Huffington Post* for $315 million, making Arianna Huffington editor-in-chief of The Huffington Post Media Group. In 2008, SMU renamed one of its oldest and most distinguished academic departments the Roy M. Huffington Department of Earth Sciences from a $10 million gift of the Huffington family.

27

The End of an Era

For companies in the marine offshore oil drilling and production business, there has been a history of feast or famine. How bad has it been? In 2000, the CEO of ExxonMobil was quoted as saying that the biggest mistake ExxonMobil made in the offshore oil business was getting into the business. He explained that, over the years, they had made no profits.

It was particularly hard for companies like Levingston. When a boom started, as the leader in their field, they would be the first shipyard to get new orders. As the boom progressed, their shipyard would be tied up with work and they were forced to turn down new jobs. This meant they would miss business where customers were willing to pay top prices. When the boom was over, they were caught with too much overhead. Levingston had made a strategic mistake in gearing their business to new rig construction. They missed repairs for tugs and barges for the intercostal transportation industry and special fabrications for the petrochemical industry. Levingston did no new construction of warships, except for the four Corvettes for the Iranian Navy in the mid-1960's.

Beginning in the early 1970's, several internal changes occurred at Levingston that forever altered the company's fate. The departure of long-time Levingston president Ed Malloy, in 1972, and the shake-up of the board of directors spelled the end of an era for the shipyard, and started the company down a path from which it never fully recovered.

In mid-1972, the company announced that it would have to report a net loss on its investments for the previous year, a fact which it attributed to cost overruns on several major contracts. The company also bought Gulfport Shipyard in Port Arthur which, incidentally, helped to keep Levingston afloat with repair contracts during the trying financial times of the ensuing decade. The company's fortunes changed in 1975 when Ashland Oil purchased Levingston Shipbuilding Co. after more than a year of merger negotiations. The change in ownership and subsequent financial strains resulted in a slow decline for the company. It simply could not sustain the "oil bust" that would strike in the 1980's. A forerunner in the offshore construction industry and a symbol of pride to the residents of Orange, Levingston continued building and repairing offshore marine vessels until the downturn of the early 1980's forced the shipyard to close.

In the first couple of years of the 1980's, shipyards across the Gulf Coast struggled to keep pace with the enormous volume of new rig and platform orders and deliveries. High day rates and high oil prices produced a boom in the Gulf of Mexico that had continued since the late 1970's. However, by 1982, the number of new rigs, platforms, and Offshore Service Vessels (OSVs) that entered the market outstripped the industry's demand for them. By 1984, the worldwide demand for oil had dropped and the oil rig market was oversaturated. Levingston, like many other Gulf Coast firms, was caught in the crosshairs. Although the company quickly faded from the scene, its legacy continues to live on in the fabrication yards of the Golden Triangle that arose from the ashes of the great oil bust.

In the early 1970's, several tragedies befell the Levingston family. In 1971, Bob Murphy, the nephew of Ed Malloy's deceased wife, "Baby," was accidentally killed when a garage door at his home fell on him. Murphy was being groomed to take over the leadership of Levingston. That following year, Ed Malloy suffered an illness and essentially left the company. He died in early 1973, leaving a gaping hole in the leadership. "Old Man Ed" had been part of the core group that came together at Levingston during World War II. The death of Malloy ended an era of a man whose business career was built on honesty, integrity, and on building relationships based on trust. Like many from his generation, Malloy had a drinking problem that impaired his energy level as he got older. However, he always commanded the respect from the Levingston team to follow him when he made a decision.

The controlling stock fell to the hands of three widows: Marjorie Malloy, the widow of Ed Malloy; Collette Malloy, Frank's widow; and Ollie Pennington, whose husband died October 18, 1967, while president of Levingston. George W. Brown, Jr., who had been the company's attorney since the World War II days, was named chairman of the board. Ed Malloy's heirs had an in-law named Bob Jones who wanted to take control of the company. Jones saw the existing executive leadership of Levingston as a threat to his plans. Larry Baker, for instance, had successfully run the overseas venture in Singapore. With the stroke of his pen, Jones fired the three long-time top executives—George W. Brown Jr., attorney; Malcolm Vaughan, president; and Larry Baker, Far East Levingston general manager. Consequently, the shipbuilder's bankers went into a panic and demanded that Levingston hire someone to run the company. Jones, in response, hired a local retired banker to run Levingston and to market it for sale.

Built in 1975, the *Glomar Java Sea* was a sister ship of the *Glomar Challenger* and part of the Grand Island-class, deep-sea drillships, eight of which were built at Levingston. It was designed for international waters leased by ARCO (Atlantic Richfield Co.), which was later acquired in the year 2000 by BP Amoco.

The U.S. Coast Guard reports that on October 25, 1983, at 23:48 local time, the Assistant Rig Manager, onboard the *Glomar Java Sea*, called Global Marine's office in Houston and reported that the drillship had a fifteen-degree starboard list of unknown origin and was experiencing seventy-five-knot winds over the bow. Communications were cut off during the conversation, and all attempts to reestablish contact failed. Five minutes later, at about 23:51, the *Glomar Java Sea* capsized and within minutes sank in 317 feet of water. The *Java Sea* crew, with eighty-one persons onboard was gone, no survivors. She sank in the South China Sea at a position approximately sixty-three nautical miles southwest of Hainan Island, People's Republic of China and eighty nautical miles east of the Socialist Republic of Vietnam.

Prior to the sinking, the *Glomar Java Sea* had secured drilling operations due to the severe effects of tropical storm LEX approaching from the east of the drilling site.

An extensive search was conducted. A diving expedition found the wreck in an inverted position approximately 1,600 feet southwest of the good site that it was drilling. Probably no other marine disaster has been more thoroughly researched, and it is still studied by the offshore world. The disaster was rare in that there were no survivors ever found. Of the 81 aboard, 45 remain unaccounted for. Thirty-six bodies were found in the wreckage. The results have been the making of many changes in operating procedures and engineering. The actual causes are still unknown.

Larry Kelley, the purchasing agent for the construction of the *Java Sea* at Levingston, has a theory for the sinking. He offered the possibility that the anchors in the seafloor broke on one side and the vessel was thrown over by a wave.

Charles H. "Buddy" King, a retired offshore marine executive of Global Marine (now called Transocean), kept a plaque on his office wall with the names of the crew who perished. The tragedy impacted everyone in the offshore drilling community. When the *Glomar Java Sea* was built in the late 1970's, Global knew it would be used all over the world. They went all out in having the best equipment and systems that were available. The offshore rig businesses, together with the suppliers and customers, have worked very hard to ensure that the men lost aboard *Glomar Java Sea* did not die in vain.

As previously noted, eighty-one persons were aboard the *Glomar Java Sea;* thirty-six bodies were found and forty-five persons remain missing and presumed dead. One lifeboat had been launched and was found three days later, having capsized. Prevailing sea currents from the site went west towards Vietnam, about eighty miles. The evidence indicated that the lifeboat had been properly launched and lowered. There were reports of surviving crew members with sightings in Vietnamese jails. These reports have never been substantiated. Another theory is that they escaped from the *Glomar Java Sea* in a lifeboat and were captured by Vietnamese military forces. There have been differing theories on what caused the ship to capsize.

Thousands of people had served on the *Glomar Java Sea* or been involved in some way in the building and operations of the ship.

"The offshore oil industry was plunged into profound grief by definite news of the stupendous loss of life caused by the wreck of Glomar Java. (The Offshore Oil, October 25, 1983)

Back in Orange, the grief was widespread among the shipyard workers who had worked on building the *Glomar Java Sea*. Paranoia set in. Was it something they had done wrong in engineering or in construction? Since the ship ended up on the water's bottom in only 357 feet of water, the investigators could survey the damage.

The site Oilrigphotos.com (http://www.oilrig-photos.com/picture/number1760.asp) includes some blogs about the tragedy.

One blogger wrote, "I put it away for over thirty years and now I can't leave it alone. When I made my first post in Oct 14, I went home and cried like a baby. My wife didn't know what to think. Once she saw all these posts she understood how much of a family everyone was. Many of these people were children when the *Java Sea* went down, and it's awesome that they show interest in wanting to really know what happened."

In April 1981, the price of crude oil in the United States had hit a peak of $36.95 per barrel. During this time, the oil industry suffered a mass delusion that the price of oil would continue to rise indefinitely. There was a popular saying in Houston: "Fifty dollars by 1985." The oil people were in the mother lode of a gold strike, and it was going to get even better, many predicted. By April 1986, however, the price had precipitously dropped, reaching as low as under $10.00 a barrel. The Texas-Louisiana Gulf Coast economy was devastated, and the oil industry went into a bust, taking with it commercial and residential real estate and many banks.

Thousands were thrown out of work. In January 1983, unemployment in the six-county Houston metropolitan area rose to 9.1 percent, the highest among the state's biggest metropolitan areas. Beaumont-Port Arthur was hit even harder, with a rate of 14.9 percent. The overall rate for Texas was 8.5 percent. With a few exceptions, nearly every major bank in Texas was closed, sold to, or merged with West Coast or East Coast banking groups. The New York bankers danced with joy. The law disallowing any banks outside the state of Texas from owning a bank in Texas was repealed. Almost $100 billion of Texas bank assets failed from 1980 to 1994.

In 1985, almost ten million barrels of oil were produced each day. Saudi Arabia cut back production to a low of 3 million barrels that year, then raised it up to 8 million barrels a day in 1986, ramping up to 9.6 million in 2015.

28

Rocket 88

In the car business, General Motors launched its feverish drive for high performance, gas-guzzling engines in 1949 with the overhead valve V-8 Oldsmobile engine named "Rocket 88." It is recognized as the first of the muscle cars. They followed up with the V-8 engine for the 1955 Chevrolet and the Corvette. The race was on to build the biggest, most powerful cars. The automotive fever with tailfins, lots of chrome, and big, powerful engines was exploited and led by GM. The fever affected the entire petroleum industry. It meant more gasoline needed to be produced with a higher-octane rating. This was the start of Americans slurping leaded gas through massive V-8 engines. In the New York headquarters of the world's largest petroleum company—Standard Oil of New Jersey—its president, Monroe Jackson "Jack" Rathbone, felt these pressures. "Gene Holtzman, Chairman of Jersey at the time, was a friend of Alfred E. Sloane, Jr.," Rathbone recalls. Sloane was the iconic leader of General Motors. "I asked Mr. Sloane why Detroit didn't make a low-cost car with high mileage for young married people." Mr. Sloane didn't like that. "I know so much more than you as to what the average American motorists wants that your question is presumptuous." He growled. "Six months later," Rathbone added, "the first Volkswagen Beetle appeared in the United States, and the Germans sold 500,000 of them before some tinkering with the import rates slowed the flood." Rathbone was Jersey's president from 1954–1963 and Chairman from 1963–1965.

When the Standard Oil Company (New Jersey) and the Humble Oil & Refining Company changed its name to Exxon Corporation, it was 1972. It is hard to believe that General Motors was ranked as the largest corporation in the world. Exxon was number two. Today, the only U.S.-based automobile manufacturer left from those "glory days" is Ford - that is, those which haven't been sold to foreign auto companies, filed bankruptcy (General Motors), or just flat gone out of business. Why did Detroit make super-powered heavy gas-guzzling vehicles for everyday use? The quote from Rathbone answers the question. A common answer for the managers in Detroit is the claim that big, powerful cars were easier to sell and more profitable. Maybe this philosophy is why Detroit no longer reigns as the king of the automobile industry. One automobile guru calls it the ultimate example of arrogance and greed of industry leaders. This was the start of Americans devouring leaded gas through massive V-8 engines.

The Oldsmobile was no more in 2004. Some credit Jackie Brenton's 'Rocket 88' recording from 1951 as the first rock and roll song. It certainly had the correct elements; it was about a car - a 1950 Oldsmobile 88 with a high-compression, overhead-valve Rocket V-8 engine. The song is also notable because it featured Ike Turner on keyboards. At one time, the Old's Cutlass was the most popular model of all U.S. cars. The last Oldsmobile, rolled off an assembly line on April 29, 2004 in Lansing, Michigan

The Volkswagen Beetle became part of the cultural pattern of America, and they still sell a modernized version. The quotes from Rathbone were taken from *The Professional, A Biography of JB Saunders* by Otto J. Scott (1976).

In 1960, a Volkswagen Beetle could be bought for $1,720, including tax, title and license. My brother, Joe, was selling Volkswagons and remembers the sales price. My wife, Carole, bought a 1961 model Beetle in 1962 at the start of her teaching career with the the Houston Independent School District. It included neither air conditioning nor gas gauge. "Twice I ran out of gas coming through the Texas Medical Center area on my way home from Cullen Junior High School, located on Scott Street. Both times my father, John Stevens, came to my aid with a filled gas can," says Carole.

The mileage of the VW was about thirty-five miles per gallon. Compare that to a Chevy with a big V-8 engine, costing some $2,500 and consuming some ten miles per gallon. If you averaged 10,000 miles per year, your fuel cost at $0.30 cents per gallon for the consumed 1,000 gallons would be $300. To drive the same distance with a Beetle would cost $115.80 for only 386 gallons. Back in those days, when the average annual wages were about $7,500, that was a real savings.

The last year that the United States was self-sufficient in oil was 1949. From that point, the United States became a net importer of oil. Most of the excess, wasteful gasoline produced to keep the American gas guzzler driving came from imported oil, which demands high military costs to keep the oil lanes secure. The oil industry had to make deals with nations for their oil to bring to America for the high-octane Detroit folks. Not only did they have to expand oil refineries, but they had to invest more money in their refineries to process the high-octane gasoline for the high-powered engines.

When the American public complains about their automobile fuel costs, Detroit is quick to blame it on the high price of gasoline charged by the oil industry. The auto industry has politically lobbied for no increase in the federal sales tax charge on gasoline. It has not been raised since the Omnibus Budget Reconciliation Act of 1993, signed by President Bill Clinton on August 10 of that year, increased the gas tax to 18.4 cents per gallon. The money goes to the Highway Trust Fund.

29

The Final Days of Levingston

In 1975, unexpectedly, Ashland Oil stepped up and bought Levingston for stock valued at $25 million. Everyone at the company thought the magic would quickly return like in the "good old days." To the contrary, Ashland's first move was to hire Edward Earl Paden, a young executive from the East Coast with Naval shipbuilding experience, to run the business. Unfortunately, Paden had no experience in the offshore marine business, and neither did the people he hired to help run the company. The main ingredients in the offshore marine business are trust and integrity. It was a different world from building ships for the Navy, which is fraught with the political pressures brought to bear by local congressmen. In the offshore oil business, contracts were loosely drawn. Your word was your bond, never to be tarnished. It was a cooperative environment between the ship builders, rig operators, and the oil companies. In time, Paden's lack of experience in the offshore construction market began to influence the company's financial outlook.

In October 1978, Ashland agreed to back Levingston in a $200 million dollar contract to build five 32,000 ton dry-bulk carriers. Ashland took an equity position in the ownership of the ships in order to make the deal go through. Many observers thought that was an unwise business move. Building a dry-bulk carrier in a drilling rig yard was like building a Ford Fusion in a BMW plant.

Two years later, Ashland sold Levingston to Ed Paden for $26 million. The bank of Nova Scotia and Rhode Island Hospital Trust financed the deal with partial guarantees by Ashland. During December of 1980, the prime interest rate hit 21.50 percent.

A year later, Paden bought Sun Shipbuilding Co. for a purchase price of $12 million that was financed by Sun Oil Company, now Sunoco. He renamed it Pennsylvania Shipyard. This was a shipyard that had a reported $200 million in net worth a few years before the sale and then a reported loss of $68 million the year after the sale. Paden immediately and aggressively went after Navy work by opening an office in Anapolis, Maryland.

Sun Oil, original owner of the shipyard, was controlled by the Pew Family, one of the wealthiest families in America. They had made their fortune in the Spindletop oilfield in Beaumont, Texas. The Pew family is famous for their contributions and research with the Pew Charitable Trust, an independent, nonprofit, nongovernmental organization founded in 1948, which now has over $5 billion in assets.

A contract to construct fleet oilers for the Navy was awarded to Penn Ship in 1985 and subsequently terminated when cash flow problems prevented completion. From 1988 to 1994, various government agencies conducted approximately seventeen investigations of this contract, in whole or part with no action against Pennsylvania Shipping Company. For the next few years, the shipyard skated along with little or no activity. Paden, as owner of Levingston, had tried to diversify into federal government work, while at the same time abandoning the offshore marine business and even the custom fabrication for the local petrochemical and refinery industries, which had been the company's bread and butter for decades. Levingston was overleveraged with debt. Then, one day in 1985, the steam whistle sounded for the last time at the Levingston shipyard. The blast of the steam whistle, signifying a shift change at the yard, was the sound of the "glory days." Every day at five o'clock, a shift change whistle shrieked across town. A few minutes later, the front gate of the yard would swarm with an assortment of folks heading for one of the parking lots and eventually home. It was a big part of life in Orange. Everything from street traffic to retail sales was affected by the patterns of the shift change. The shift change that occurred in 1986 would be the last for Levingston.

In the end, it was not the workers or foreign competition that led to the demise of Levingston. It was misguided leadership in the middle of a global market collapse in offshore oil drilling in the early 1980's. When the price of oil plunged, the oil and gas companies stopped calling for drilling rigs. Then drilling companies, in turn, stopped ordering new rigs. It was a similar pattern of perpetual boom-and-bust in the oilfield that had repeated itself many times before, and will likely continue to do so in the future. But this time, the downswing was especially severe. A core sector of Levingston's business was essentially wiped out. Moreover, Paden's financial troubles in the ship business on the East Coast were tied to the fortunes of Levingston. Paden was forced into bankruptcy, and he subsequently liquidated Levingston and then Penn Ship.

The demise of Levingston was a tragic mistake. It is a part of the industry's dark side.

30

David W. Hannah, Jr.

Early in 1982, Daniel Yergin, author of *The Prize,* said that the talk of oil spiking to $100 a barrel, as was much being predicted, was premature. Prices, which had skyrocketed from $3 a barrel to $36, thanks to the oil crisis of the 1970's, crashed in 1986. The cause of the crash is generally believed to be the actions of Saudi Arabia. They began their oil production in 1939. By 1949 the production was up to 500,000 barrels per day. Production increased to almost 10 million barrels per day in 1980. By 1985, Saudi Arabia was down to less than 3 million barrels per day, down from the peak level of 10 million barrels per day. At the time, the global oil demand was about 60 million barrels per day. A drop of 8 million barrels was 13% of global demand. Based on 2015, demand of 93 million barrels per day global demand, a 13% drop would be about 12 million barrels. King Fahd made the decision to ramp up oil production. Saudi Arabia quickly brought their production back up in a matter of months and oil prices collapsed. It caught the oilmen in the world by complete surprise. They had forgotten that Saudi Arabia had merely cut back on their oil production. They could quickly turn the valves back on and produce. The high oil price was not based on true demand and supply economics.

As the oil industry collapsed, the Federal Reserve Banking took the position of punishing the Texas banks. Rather than cutting the banks some slack on their loans, they clamped down on the Texas banks, forcing many into bankruptcy and others were forced to sell to the large national banks. Only a few small banks and two large regional banks, Victoria Bancshares and Cullen Frost Bank survived without the shareholders losing control. The U.S. domestic oil industry leaders had failed to consider a possibility which turned out to truly be a "black sheep" event for the oil exploration and production industry.

For some background about what it was like during that period, David Hannah, the race director (1980–2002) of the Houston Marathon, now sponsored by Chevron, told me the story about Tenneco Inc., based in Houston. They were the first Houston Marathon sponsor. Hannah asked Jim Ketelson, Tenneco CEO, in January 1986 to sponsor the U.S. trials for the Olympic marathon to be held in South Korea. The cost was estimated at one million to sponsor. Ketelson told Hannah that Tenneco would provide the money. At the time, oil was selling for $28 per barrel. Hannah started preparation for the bid. Only two months later, the price of oil dropped to $10 per barrel. The sharp decline in crude oil price was caused by Saudi Arabia's decision to reform its petroleum policy and to increase production. Similarly, the large oil price increase between 1979 and 1981 usually is attributed to an internal policy change by OPEC. The wild price changes left no doubt that the oil cartel lead by Saudi Arabia controlled the price of oil. Tenneco informed Hannah that they would have to renege on the $1 million commitment. At the time, Tenneco was ranked as one of the top twenty-five companies in America. Stories like this were repeated in the oil patch.

Then, in October 1987, the stock market fell by 20 percent. This was only the fourth time that the market had dropped more than 20 percent since 1926. What caused it? Theories abound, but no one could come up with strong proof. All of this combined with the surprise of the oil price collapse to wreck the economy. One oil man explained what happened saying, "When the music, plays you have to dance."

31

College Students and Levingston

In 1972, more than 120 college students worked during the summer at Levingston to help pay for their college educations. Don Martell told me a story about working under Don Covington in the engineering department. In the summer of 1965, Martell was home from Texas A & M University, where he played football and majored in architectural construction science. Martell was following in his brother, Ron's, footsteps at Texas A&M and working summers at Levingston.

Martell tells the story of when he and a friend were not doing their best while working in the air-conditioned engineering office. One evening, their boss, Don Covington, told them to dress in old, cool clothing the next day, as they would be working out in the hot shipyard. Covington assigned them to outdoor work for a week before letting them come back inside to their job in the engineering building. Martell says Covington got his message across: no goofing off on the job while working for him. Covington was known as a strong leader who particularly enjoyed mentoring young people. Martell also says that Levingston was paying him $2.25 an hour, which was substantially higher than any of his classmates at Texas A&M enjoyed for summer work. Hiring college students in the summer was an unofficial company policy at Levingston.

Martell also tells the story of bringing his father, Bob Martell, to the christening party of a drill barge for Santa Fe Drilling. It was particularly exciting to meet Kuwaiti businessmen in their native dress. Kuwait Drilling Company had become a joint venture partner with Santa Fe. Both companies are now part of Transocean Drilling.

Ron Martell, Don's brother, was recruited by Bum Phillips, the freshman coach under Bear Bryant at Texas A&M. Phillips had been the coach at Nederland High School and knew Ron's athletic ability. Bum's sister, Adrina Ingram, and her husband Ralph, were close friends of my parents. It was she who gave her brother his nickname of "Bum." I remember her as a gorgeous woman. When I would see Bum on TV as coach of the Houston Oilers, I would think to myself that she had captured all the good looks in that family. Bum Phillips is the eighth winningest coach in NFL history. He was, said one admirer, the "Will Rogers of the NFL," justly famous for such sayings as, "There's two kinds of coaches: them that's been fired, and them that's gonna be fired."

Jerry Pennington was another college student who worked at the shipyard. He was the nephew of Walter Pennington and worked three years at Levingston helping to pay his way through law school. Today he is the Municipal Court Judge in Orange, Texas.

Retired District Judge, Pat Allen Clark, spent five summers at Levingston working to help pay for his education. Clark gets emotional when he talks about how important that job was for his education. Clark's father was an employee of Levingston. The Orange County Texas Exes, of which Clark is a former president, proudly announced in 2010 the creation of the Judge Patrick A. Clark Endowed Academic Scholarship. This endowed scholarship is given each year to an Orange County high school senior who excels in community service and will attend the University of Texas as a freshman.

Dick Selby was another Orange student who worked at Levingston while attending Texas A&M. Selby earned an electrical engineering degree, and after a stint in the Air Force, retired from Martin and Lockheed.

At Levingston, Selby worked in the engineering, drafting, and design department and remembers the beautiful handwork in the drawings that were produced there. Today drafters use computer-aided design (CAD) systems where the computer does the drawing. The teacher of mechanical drawing at Orange High school, who had lost a leg in the Korean War, also worked part-time in the Levingston engineering drafting department.

Willie "Will" Bednar worked several summers at Levingston while attending Texas A&M. Will was the son of Peter Bednar, who retired as Vice President of Engineering at Levingston.

Larry David, a member of a pioneer Orange family and a prominent civic leader, experienced working at Levingston in his youth. David worked summers at Levingston while attending college. The work was physically demanding in the heat and humidity of the shipyard environs. He performed his job alongside many hardworking Cajuns. One morning, when he walked through the front gates at the shipyard, he noticed that hardly anyone was in the yard. Larry was not aware of any holiday, so he asked what was wrong. The guard at the gate laughed and told David it was the first day of shrimping season. Levingston gladly adapted to local patterns and customs allowing workers to take leaves of absence.

Today, David is on the board of directors of the Edward Timothy Malloy Foundation which has $6.5 million assets that support three charities in Orange: St. Mary's Catholic School, the Methodist Church, and the Red Cross. They issue three equal checks each year. He is also Chairman of the Board of the Stark Foundation which has around half a billion dollars in assets. David and my wife, Carole, are distant cousins through his mother's Dullahan family.

Guy Covington, who grew up in the shipyard culture, explained its importance: "It was the center of the known universe, as far as we were concerned, Levingston Shipbuilding. My mother just—I mean, she didn't remember eating a meal that didn't come from Levingston. And her whole family worked there. And my whole family worked there, you know. We thought that everybody that worked anywhere else was just killing time, that this was the only real business in the world. It was a unique feeling. There was a lot of pride. You were instantly friends with anybody else you met whose father worked at Levingston, you know. I remember I played Little League football. There were four of us on my Little League team who had either a father or mother working at Levingston, and we were in the *Levingston News Log*, which was published once a month or whatever. We had our pictures in there because we were all going to Florida for the National Little League Championship. Had our pictures in the *Levingston News Log*! It was important."

32

Conclusion

Larry Baker, Sr. told me that the main thing he learned at Levingston was that leadership matters. He described good leadership with this quote from Thomas Paine, one of the Founding Fathers of the United States: "Lead, follow, or get out of the way." I thought, it can't be much simpler than that. Working at the shipyard was hard, hot, dirty, and noisy, with danger that made it no easy life. The success of Levingston was due to highly skilled individual performers, rather than one strong leader.

Since the first oil was produced in 1859, when Edwin Drake drilled the first oil well in Titusville, Pennsylvania, the world has consumed about 1,400 billion barrels for transportation, power plants, and plastics. At the rate of consumption in 2015, which was about ninety million barrels a day or roughly thirty-three billion barrels for the year, we will use the same amount in the next forty-two years. No one knows how much we will produce in the future. But we do know that the oil pioneers have made fantastic progress with ideas and methods to rely on.

Probably the biggest difference in designing and building new things today is the speed and memory storage of the computer. The computer gives us unbelievable data and graphics in answers to our questions, but it does not ask them. The boldness and vision of early pioneers was often based on pure intellect and seat-of-the-pants judgments, often struggling with the chance of failure while seeking

In his popular book, *Outliers: The Story of Success*, Malcolm Gladwell suggests that most people's accomplishments result in significant part from interactions and help from other people and institutions. Thus, he argues, we should be modest about taking too much personal credit for our successes. The stories in this book create a poster for that observation. Anybody, who says he is self-made is a fool.

It was people like Larry Baker, Sr., who made a major contribution to the success of Levingston. And companies like Levingston played no small part in developing the technology and marine equipment that has become so vital to our world. Again and again, we know as we study history that a small act can sometimes make a change in our lives. The question we need to ask ourselves is not "Can one person make a difference?" The question we need to ask ourselves is, "What kind of a difference can I make?"

Baker, who was a fixture in the Oil Patch and a major player in marine offshore drilling, once concluded an interview with Ken Stickney for the *Times of Acadiana* (Lafayette, LA, March 29, 2015) with this simple statement: "Levingston was one helluva of a company. And that is how the little shipyard in Orange, Texas, should be remembered."

Partial List of Bibliography

Aid, Matthew. *Project Azorian: The CIA's Declassified History of the Glomar Explorer.* National Security Archives, The George Washington Archives Nuclear Vault. Posted February 12, 2010.

Alley, R. B. *The Two-Mile Time Machine: Ice Cores, Abrupt Climate Change, and Our Future.* Princeton University Press, 2000.

Alley, R.B. *Earth, The Operators' Manual.* Norton, 2011

Atkins, Annette. *Creating Minnesota: A History from the Inside Out.* Minnesota: Minnesota Historical Society, 2010.

Austin, Diane, and Drexel Woodson, eds. "Gulf Coast Communities and the Fabrication and Shipbuilding Industry." *OCS Study BOEM* 2014–610.

Beaudoin, Y. C., Dallimore, S. R., and Boswell, R. (eds.). *Frozen Heat: A UNEP Global Outlook on Methane Gas Hydrates.* Volume 2. United Nations Environment Programme, GRID-Arendal, 2014.

Bascom, Willard. *A Hole in the Bottom of the Sea.* London: Weidenfield & Nicolson, 1961.

Ballard, R. D. *The Eternal Darkness.* Princeton Legacy Library, 2000.

Beaumont Enterprise. "A Pair of Ships from Orange Used in Patrol. www.beaumontenterprise.com/news/article/A-pair-of-ships-from-Orange-used-in-patrol-for-3364159.php#ixzz2IGx3gRNk.

Bernays, Edward. *Propaganda,* H. Liveright, 1928

Bernstein, Peter L. Against the Gods—The Remarkable Story of Risk. John Wiley & Sons, 1996.

Briggs, Peter. *200,000,000 Years beneath the Seas.* New York: Holt, Rinehart, 1972.

Broecker, W. S. "Climatic Change—*Are We on Brink of a Pronounced Global Warming?"* Science New Series Vol. 189 (4201)1975.

Brown, Clair. "Historical Commentary on the District of Vegetation in Louisiana, and Some Recent Observations." *Proceedings, Louisiana Academy of Sciences,* 1943.

Burchard, Peter. *The Carol Moran,* Macmillan, 1958.

Burrough, Bryan. *The Big Rich: The Rise and Fall of the Greatest Texas Oil Fortunes.* New York: Penguin, 2010.

Chalkley, H. G. *History of the Office of the Supervisor of Shipbuilding,* USN Report 1 October 1945. Reprinted in Anahuac, Texas, *Independence.*

Cheong Colin. *CAN DO!* The Spirit of Keppel Fels Times Edition, Singapore. 2002

Churchill, Winston S. *The Hinge of Fate.* New York: Houghton Mifflin, 1950.

Cohen, Rich. *The Fish That Ate the Whale, the Life and Times of America's Banana King.* New York: Farrar, Straus and Giroux, 2012.

Coll, Steve. *Private Empire: ExxonMobil and American Power.* New York: Penguin, 2012.

Consortium for Ocean Leadership. *Marine Methane Hydrate Field Research Plan: Prepared by the Consortium for Ocean Leadership.* 2013, http://www.oceanleadership.org/scientific-programs/methane-hydrate-field-program.

Corfield, Richard. *Architects of Eternity.* Headline Book Publishing, 2001.

Corfield, Richard. *The Silent Landscape: The Scientific Voyage of* HMS Challenger. Joseph Henry Press, 2011.

Coleman, Leslie. *Can Our Free Enterprise Economy Survive?* New York: Exposition Press, 1965.

Crichton, Michael. *State of Fear.* HarperCollins, 2004.

Cornwell, Gary. *Real Answers.* Spicewood, TX: Paleface Press, 1998.

Cramer, Deborah. *Smithsonian Oceans.* Washington, DC: Smithsonian, 2008.

Craven, John P. *The Silent War.* New York: Simon and Schuster, 2001.

Cudahy, Brian J. *Over and Back: The History of Ferry Boats in New York.* Fordham University Press 1990

Davis Jim. *Memories—Stories from a Life Enjoyed Living.* Friesen Press Canada, 2014.

Davis, Wallace. *Corduroy Road, The Story of Glenn H. McCarthy.* Houston: The Anson Jones Press, 1951.

DeMenil Foundation. *Arts and Activism Projects of John and Dominique DeMenil.* Author, 2010.

Donahue, Jack. *The Finest in the Land: The Story of the Petroleum Club of Houston.* Gulf Publishing, 1984.

Douglas Joel Sikorski, *Public Enterprise in international Competition: The Case of Singapore University of Bradford, original University of Michigan 1987*

Dunham, Roger C. 1996. *Spy Sub.* Annapolis: Naval Institute Press.

Eisenhower, Dwight D. *Crusade in Europe.* Garden City, NY: Doubleday, 1948.

Ewing, Maurice. (speech, probably to BuShips). "Applications of Marine Geophysics to Military Problems, 1964," Maurice Ewing Collection, Center for American History, University of Texas at Austin, 1964 folder.

Friedman, *Thank You for Being Late* Farrar 2016

Exxon Mobil Corporation. *One Hundred Twenty-Five Years of History.* Irving, TX: Author, 2007.

Fairchild, Louis. *They Called It the War Effort: Oral Histories from World War II, Orange, Texas.* Austin: Eakin Press, 1993.

Falgoux, Woody. *Rise of the Cajun Mariner.* Stockard James, 2007.

*50 Years of Ocean Discovery. National Research Council 1950-*2000, National Academy Press, 2000

Fest, Joachim C. *Hitler.* New York: Harcourt Brace Jovanovich, New York, 1973. (Slavic people as subhuman and Einsattzgruppen)

50 Years of Offshore Oil & Gas Development. Hart Publications, 1997.

Gault, Owen. *ATA: Size Didn't Matter! Size! The Auxiliary Tugs of WW II. SEA Classics* magazine, January 2010.

Gladwell, Malcolm. *Outlier:* Outliers: The Story of Success is the third non-fiction book written by Malcolm Gladwell and published by Little, Brown and Company on November 18, 2008.

Glomar Java Sea, O.N. 568182. *Capsizing and Sinking in the South China Sea, on 25 October 1983 with Multiple Loss of Life.* Washington DC: Coast Guard, 1985.

General Motors Corporation. Proposal for Dynamic Ship Positioning System submitted to Global Marine. June 1967, P67-26.

Geophysics in the Affairs of Mankind., Tulsa: Society of Exploration Geophysicists, 2001.

Goldstein, Edward. *NASA's Earth Science Program,* Imaging Notes, Denver: Blueline Publishing LLC, Fall 2007.

Halberstam, David. *The Best and the Brightest.* Ballantine Books, 1993.

Hansen, James et al., "Global Climate Changes as Forecasted by Goddard Institute for Space Studies Three-Dimensional Model," *Journal of Geophysical Research*, Aug. 20, 1988

Hess, H. H. "The AMSOC Hole to the Earth's Mantle." *American Scientist 48* June 1960.

Hughes Glomar Explorer: Two books have been written about the project: Clyde W. Burleson, *The Jennifer Project* (Englewood Cliffs, N.J.: Prentice-Hall, 1977); and Roy Varner and Wayne Collier, *A Matter of Risk* (New York: Random House, 1977).

Hsu, Kenneth J. *Challenger at Sea, A Ship That Revolutionized Earth Science.* Princeton University Press. 1983.

Hsu, Kenneth J. *The Great Dying.* 1986.

Hsu, Kenneth J. *The Mediterranean Was a Desert.* 1982.

Jacobs, Arthur D. *The Prison Called Hohensberg.* Boca Raton, FL: Universal, 1999.

Hawking, Stephen. *A Brief History of Time.* Bantam, 1988.

Huie, William B. *CAN DO! The Story of the Seabees.* Bluejacket Books, 1997.

Intergovernmental Panel on Climate Change. *Climate Change 2001: The Scientific Basis.* Cambridge University Press, 2001.

Jacobson, Annie. *The Pentagon's Brain*. Little, Brown & Co., 2015.

King, William R. *King of Sea Diamonds: The Saga of Sam Collins*. Zeekoeviei, South Africa: Flesch Publications, 1996.

Krammer Arnold, Undue Process*: the Untold Story of American's German Alien Internees,* Maryland: Rowman and Littlefield Publishers, Inc. 1997 Laverne, Christine. *Drill Me a Painting.* Biarritz: Atlantica, 2008.

Laborde, Alden J. *My Life and Times*. Laborde Printing, 1997.

Lichtblau, Eric. *The Nazis Next Door.* New York: Houghton, NY 2014.

Lim, Richard. *Tough Men, Bold Visions: The Story of Keppel.* Singapore: Keppel, 1993.

Lindsey and Rienstra. *Beaumont: A Chronicle of Promise.* Windsor, 1982.

McCann, Thomas P. *An American Company: The Tragedy of United Fruit.* New York: Crown, 1976.

McNary, J. F., Person, A., and Ozudogru, Y. H. "A 7,500-Ton-Capacity, Shipboard, Completely Gimbaled and Heave-Compensated Platform." *Journal of Petroleum Technology* April 1977: 439–48.

Menard, Henry W. "Scripps Institution Oceanography, 1974." Scripps Institution of Oceanography Library (http://scilib.ucsd.edu/sio).

Munk, Walter. *Seventy Years of Exploration in Oceanography.* Springer, 2010.

National Research Council (US). AMSOC Committee. *Drilling through the Earth's Crust, Conducted by the AMSOC Committee.* September 1, 1959. Washington: National Academy of Sciences, National Research Council, 1959.

Offley, Edward. *Scorpion Down.* Highbridge, 2007

O. Henry. (William Porter) *Cabbages and Kings.* Garden City, NY: Doubleday, 1914.

Olien, Roger M., and Hinton, Diana. *Wildcatters: Texas Independent Oilmen.* Texas A & M Press, 2007.

Oristaglio, Michael, and Dorozynski, Alexander. *A Sixth Sense.* The Overlook Press, 2009.

Peebles, Robert. "Technology as a Factor in Gulf Coast Shipyards, 1900–1945." Unpublished PhD Dissertation, Denton, Texas, North Texas State University. 1980.

Perrin, Warren. *Acadie Then and Now.* Andrepoint Publishing, 2014.

Polmar, Norman. *The Death of the USS Thresher,* Lyons press 2004

Pope Francis. *Encyclical on Climate Change & Inequality.* Brooklyn: Melville House, 2015.

Pratt, Joseph A., Tyler Priest, and Christopher Castaneda. *Offshore Pioneers: Brown & Root and the History of Offshore Oil and Gas.* Houston: Gulf Publishing, 1997.

Priest, Tyler: The Offshore Imperative: Shell Oil. Series: Kenneth E. Montague Series in Oil and Business History (Book 19), 2009.

Priest, Tyler, and John Lajaunie. *Gulf Coast Communities and the Fabrication and Shipbuilding Industry: A Comparative Community Study. Volume I: Historical Overview and Statistical Model.* US Department of the Interior, Bureau of Ocean Energy Management, Gulf of Mexico OCS Region, New Orleans, LA. OCS Study BOEM 2014-609, 2014.

Prothero Donald R. *Greenhouse of the Dinosaurs Evolution, Extinction, and the Future of Our Planet.* Columbia University Press, 2009.

Richelson, Jeffrey. *A Century of Spies: Intelligence in the Twentieth Century.* New York: Oxford University Press, 1995.

Rhodes, Richard. *Arsenals of Folly.* Knopf, 2007.

Rodengen, Jeffrey. *The Legend of Noble Drilling.* Write Stuff Enterprises, 2001.

Rubino, Anna. *Queen of the Oil Club.* Beacon Press, 1992.

Russell, Jan Jarbode. *The Train to Crystal City.* Scribner, 2015.

Salmon, Patricia M. *The Staten Island Ferry: A History.* Staten Island Museum, 2008.

Scripps, San Diego, The Institution. *Dynamic Positioning for D/V Glomar Challenger.* National Information Technical Services, US Dept. of Commerce, 1971.

Secor, Laura. *Children of Paradise: The Struggle for the Soul of Iran.* New York: Riverhead Books, 2016.

Severinghaus, J. P., and E. J. Brook. "Abrupt Climate Change at the End of the Last Glacial Period Inferred from Trapped Air in Polar Ice." *Science 286*, 930–34, 1999 (doi:10.1126/science.286.5441.930).

Schefter, James L. *Santa Fe International Company: An Oil Service Company Story.* San Pedro, CA: Omega, 1990.

Schempf, F. Jay. *Pioneering Offshore: The Early Years.* Offshore Energy Center, 2007.

Schnuerle, Angela M. "The Spirit of Gulfport." Unpublished Honor Thesis, University of Houston, 1991.

Sharp, David H. *The CIA's Greatest Covert Operation: Inside the Daring Mission to Recover a Nuclear-Armed Soviet Sub.* University Press of Kansas, 2012.

Shor, Elizabeth Nobe. *Scripps Institution of Oceanography: Probing the Oceans 1936 to 1976.* San Diego: Tofua Press, 1978.

Shrock Robert R. *Cecil and Ida Green Philanthropists Extraordinary.* Massachusetts Institute of Technology, 1989.

SIO. "The Research Ship *Horizon.*" *SIO Reference* 74-3, 1974, p. 4.

Sontag, Sherry, and Christopher Drew. *Blind Man's Bluff: The Untold Story of American Submarine Espionage.* New York: Public Affairs, 1998.

Staten Island Museum. *Staten Island Ferry.* Arcadia, 2014.

Stover, John F. *American Railroads.* Chicago: The University of Chicago Press, 1997.

Strahan, Jerry E. *Andrew Jackson Higgins and the Boats That Won World War II.* Louisiana State University Press, 2011.

Stuart Ewen, PR! A Social History of Spin (New York, NY: Perseus Books, 1996), Tierney, Dominic. *FDR and the Spanish Civil War.* Duke University Press, 2007.

Tuyll, Hubert van. *Feeding the Bear: American Aid to the Soviet Union in 1941-1945.* Greenwood Press, 1989.

Tye, Larry. *The Father of Spin: Edward Bernays and the Birth of Public Relations.* New York: Holt 1998.

Urban, Erin. *Caddell Dry Dock; 100 Years harborside* Noble Maritime Collection, Staten Island, NY 2009

US Naval Institute Archives. April 10, 1963: Search for the USS Thresher

Uyeda, Seiya. *The New View of the Earth.* W.H. Freeman and Co, 1978.

Van Keuren. D. K. Drilling to the mantle: Project Mohole and federal support for the Earth sciences after Sputnik. Paper unpublished, 1995.

Verne, Jules. *Journey to the Center of the Earth* (French title *Voyage au centre de la Terre*), 1884. (1864 science fiction novel)

247

Verne, Jules. *Propeller Island*, Create Space, 2013 [first published in 1895].

Walker, Gabrielle. *Antarctica*. New York: Houghton, Mifflin, 2013.

Walraven, Bill. *Corpus Christi*. Windsor, 1982.

Ward, Nathan. *Dark Harbor*. Farrar, Strauss and Giroux, 2010.

Wiggins, Melanie. *Torpedoes in the Gulf*. Texas A&M Press, 1995.

Williams, Howard. *The Gateway to Texas: The History of Orange and Orange County*. Orange, TX: Heritage House Museum of Orange, 1988.

Wolfe, Louis. *THE Deepest Hole in the World: The Story of Project Mohole*. Putnam's Sons, 1964.

Woods, David. *How Apollo Flew to the Moon*. Springer, 2013.

World War II Chronicle. Legacy/Publications International, Ltd, 2007.

Yergin Daniel, *The Prize*. Free Press, 2010.

Yergin Daniel, *The Quest*. Penguin, 2012.

Made in the USA
San Bernardino, CA
04 March 2017